ACCLAIM FOR MARCH EGERTON'S OTHER DINING GUIDES:

Adventures in Cheap Eating: Hawaii

"A pure delight to read—full of color and unforced humor and good-natured commentary."
COLMAN ANDREWS, *LOS ANGELES TIMES*

"A lively, sometimes caustic guide . . ."
SOPHIA DEMBLING, *DALLAS MORNING NEWS*

"The funniest . . . most useful guide to come along in a long time."
SUE MCCLURE, *NASHVILLE BANNER*

"It crackles with a knowing humor born of countless encounters with Hawaii's exotic fare."
JIM WITTY, *HAWAII MAGAZINE*

Adventures in Cheap Eating: Nashville

"Whether on catfish shacks or coffeehouses, meat-&-threes or vegetarian spots, the writing is tight, funny and so good that it's a pleasure to read."
NICKI PENDLETON, *NASHVILLE BANNER*

ADVENTURES

IN

CHEAP EATING

● ● ● ● ●

Atlanta

ATLANTA
COMMUNITY
FOOD
BANK

A portion of the proceeds from this book will be donated to the Atlanta Community Food Bank.

ABOUT THE ATLANTA COMMUNITY FOOD BANK

The Chinese writer Lin Yutang once said that if a man will be sensible and one fine morning, while he is lying in bed, count at the tips of his fingers how many things in this life truly give him pleasure, invariably he will find food is the first one. The *Adventures in Cheap Eating* series of dining guides stands as testimony to the fact that we share that view.

But for many folks, just getting enough to eat every day is a struggle. The Atlanta Community Food Bank is dedicated to fighting hunger by distributing millions of pounds of food every year to area food pantries, soup kitchens, and other nonprofit agencies in metro Atlanta and North Georgia.

The ACFB provides an alternative to food waste by reclaiming and storing a variety of food products donated by retailers, wholesalers, caterers, and individuals like you. Sorted, inspected and packed by the staff and thousands of volunteers, food parcels are then distributed to those in need. The Food Bank also provides technical assistance and training for an array of community needs, such as organizing soup kitchens and neighborhood gardens.

For information on contributing your time or money to the cause, please write to the **Atlanta Community Food Bank, 970 Jefferson St. NW, Atlanta, GA 30318**. Or call the Food Bank at **404-892-9822**.

ADVENTURES
IN
CHEAP EATING
• • • • •
Atlanta

Terrific Deals and Authentic Meals
in and around Hotlanta

STEVE ROSENBERG
&
MARCH EGERTON

Atlanta, Georgia   Portland, Oregon

A WORD OF GRATITUDE AND A HEARTY HANDCLASP ARE IN ORDER
FOR THESE KIND FOLKS:

MAHAN ARCHER
PAUL DANIELS
AMY CONNAH HUDSON
DONNA ROSENBERG
KEELY SCHNEIDER-TRUOG
TOBIN TRUOG
DONNA WILLIAMS

ADVENTURES IN CHEAP EATING: ATLANTA

Cover Artwork by March Egerton
Cover Photo by Steve Rosenberg
Cover Design by Donna Rosenberg and March Egerton
Interior Design and Illustrations by March Egerton

Library of Congress Catalog Card Number: 95-62114

ISBN: 0-9637709-3-4

First Edition

Tsunami Press
P.O. Box 80151
Portland, Oregon 97280-1151

EatCheap@aol.com

for
Brooks

and

for
Nicholas and Madison

INTRODUCTION

For a city that began as a weed-choked termination point of the Western & Atlantic Railroad little more than 150 years ago, Atlanta has done alright for itself. Springing to life in the mid-1800s, the town barely got rolling before it was unceremoniously torched in 1864 by the infamous Union general, William Sherman. But like the fabled Phoenix that has since been incorporated into the official city seal, Atlanta rose from the ashes and went about resurrecting itself. It began once more to prosper, and in the years following the Civil War the city became a magnet for rural Southerners in search of opportunity—not leastly, newly emancipated slaves beginning their new lives.

The intervening decades have seen Atlanta's star continue in the ascendant, and it has long been recognized as the undisputed cultural and economic hub of the New South. In the last quarter century or so Atlanta has become a major American city; today, with its relentless pro-business attitude, the rise of Ted Turner's media empire and the coming of the 1996 Olympics, Atlanta has taken its place as a bona fide player on the world stage.

As the city's population and reputation have grown, so too have its dining prospects. Where once it was ex-slaves and sharecroppers making their way to Atlanta, these days the city's immigrants hail from around the globe. As is inevitably the case in such situations, the local cuisine has been steadily ratcheting upwards in quality as well as diversity—nowadays, you can find everything from Peruvian to Vietnamese to Cuban to Sicilian cookery, often times all in the same neighborhood. Of course, that's not to say that longstanding Georgia favorites like Brunswick stew, barbecue, biscuits and sweet potato pie (to name but a few) have lost any of their shine.

Unfortunately, what all of these *have* lost to a degree is visibility. Ours is an age where businesses rise and fall as much on their marketing strategies as the quality of their products. Hence, places which serve impeccable food at fair prices but lack glitz and an advertising budget can get lost. Conversely, to simply follow the brightest signs, as it were, can often lead to mediocre food and the hardest lesson in false economy this side of a Flowbee haircut.

The purpose of this guide, like the others in the *Adventures in Cheap Eating* series, is to arm you with the information you need not only to dine spectacularly for cheap, but to learn something about the character of the region. So whether you live here or are just in town to check out some synchronized swimming, you'll find no better resource for eating your way around one of America's most exciting cities.

THE EXPLANATION

A Definition

The term "cheap" is, of course, quite relative; for our purposes, most of the restaurants mentioned herein offer full meals for **$10 or less** (often much less). This is not to say that some of these places won't on occasion set you back more than a sawbuck per person, but as a general rule you should be able to get away for that.

A Geography Lesson

Anyone who has spent time in Atlanta has heard the joke about every street in town having "Peachtree" in the title. While it's not quite as bad as all that, things can get a bit confusing. In most cases the restaurants herein are located in or near an identifiable neighborhood, community or town. Where these aren't easily applicable, we've indicated the general area in which they're located, in reference to the city of Atlanta—i.e., Northeast Atlanta.

A Word about Money

As far as payment is concerned, be advised that the phrase "No Plastic" means credit cards are not accepted; **Visa**, **Mastercard**, and **American Express** are suitable as payment where noted. Many places also accept personal checks, but that info has been omitted since acceptance of out-of-town drafts varies considerably, and because small businesses have been known to suspend the option altogether after a rubber check or two.

A Disclaimer

Finally, please note that restaurants come and go in this town like Falcons free agents. Needless to add, this can result in a wasted trip now and again, unless you call ahead to verify that so-and-so's rib shack is still a going concern. Likewise, things like addresses, hours of operation, and prices—as if you need to be told—change with the winds. So be smart, be flexible, and don't forget to tip.

A MAN HATH NO BETTER THING UNDER THE SUN, THAN TO EAT, AND TO DRINK, AND TO BE MERRY.

Ecclesiastes 8:15

THE TERMINUS OF THAT RAILROAD WILL NEVER BE ANYTHING MORE THAN AN EATING HOUSE.

future mayor James M. Calhoun
describing the town that later became Atlanta

ACE BARBECUE BARN & TAXI STAND

BARBECUE

Make sure you've got a navigator and an extra 15 minutes when heading to Ace for the first time. After negotiating a maze of one-way streets, you'll know you're in the right place when you see a cluster of unoccupied cabs and a line of regulars crowding the entrance. Though they may look benign enough, these folks are the competition; they routinely pack the dining room as soon as the doors open and have been known to create a run on barbecue by noon.

This pell-mell assemblage of eaters and taxis can take its toll on the parking situation, but it's worth walking a block or three for Ace's melt-in-your-mouth chopped pork, meaty Brunswick stew, and astounding beef rib sandwiches (somewhat misnamed, they're comprised of four hefty ribs tossed onto two slices of white bread). Of particular note is the tangy barbecue sauce, a thick admixture liberally applied to all sandwiches. Expect to start a little kitchen controversy when inquiring as to the sauce's creator; at least two employees claim to have invented it. Let 'em squabble while you snag extra bread for mopping up every drop.

Plate lunch options include five or six vegetables and about that many hot entrees. Daily specials are well done, ranging from chicken and dumplings to a large and wrinkly smoked pig's ear. The house specialty is a "split": a hot sausage,

30 Bell St.
Downtown
404-659-6630
11:30a-4:30a Daily
No Plastic

About *27,000* years ago, according to paleontologists, man discovered fire. Later that same day, along about suppertime, it's very likely that he invented barbecue.

Greg Johnson and
Vince Staten
Real Barbecue (1988)

sliced lengthwise, grilled and topped with chili and cheese. It's damn tasty, and as good an explanation as there is for why we have Tagamet. If meat fails to get your flag to flapping, though, the vegetable plate is piled high and a swell bargain at under $3.

Despite the undersized dining room, lunch turnover is generally brisk enough to allow for an open seat or two. One booth is directly under a poster-sized picture of a bloodied Emilio Estevez, who stopped in for a bite while filming *Freejack* ("a mindless actioner," in the estimation of Leonard Maltin). Although the waitresses don't always convey it, the restaurant's motto is "Attitude is Everything." So order up and check your receipt for a red star—if you get one, your meal is free. You can well imagine how often that happens.

AGNES AND MURIEL'S

COMFORT FOOD

1514 MONROE DRIVE
MIDTOWN
404-885-1000
11A-11P MON-THU
11A-12A FRI
10A-12A SAT
10A-11P SUN
V/MC/AMEX

Located in a converted little two-story house near Ansley Mall, Agnes and Muriel's combines a fun fifties atmosphere with a menu that likewise harkens to a time before fat grams and beta carotene passed for suitable table topics. Though the decor can at times leave you half-expecting Barbara Billingsley to come swishing around the corner in pearls and pumps (and a dress, of course), the prevailing mood is informal, with Christmas tree lights in the entryway and mismatched dishes. At peak times the tightly packed dining room takes on the chaotic but ultimately comforting feel of a family holiday dinner.

While perusing the menu you can nibble on their crispy herb bread that's reminiscent of melba toast. If a first course is in the plans, your prime option is the chicken noodle soup, with its unusually dark and flavorful stock. If that doesn't ring your bell, opt for the crabcake starter—silver-dollar sized croquettes dosed with black pepper. Entreewise, the Louisiana barbecue shrimp over grits (baked in a cayenne butter) and the pork T-bones with apple fritters rate as something of a well-chosen splurge ($13-$15), but you can also find happiness with most of the sub-$8 main courses. Any of the pasta dishes will do the trick, as will the sublime salmon pot pie, which features a lightly dilled cream sauce and plenty of potatoes, carrots and green beans.

WHAT IS A ROOFLESS CATHEDRAL COMPARED TO A WELL-BUILT PIE?

William Maginn
(1793-1842)

Among the sandwiches, best bets (all about $6.50) are the Day After Thanksgiving (roast turkey on wheat, prepared with cornbread dressing, whole cranberry sauce and field greens); the half-pound barbecue burger with cheddar and green onions; and onion parmesan bread slathered with a feta cheese spread and topped with roasted eggplant, sweet onions, carrots and yellow squash. Yow. For veggies on the side, watch for cornmeal-battered fried green tomatoes, collard greens cooked with lemon juice and sesame seeds, and the shoestring-cut fried sweet potatoes. Unless the words "Green Goddess" send your pulse galloping, we'll likely be in agreement that the salads are best left alone.

Desserts are pricey ($4-$5) but huge. Besides the wholly terrific banana pudding (topped with toasted cinnamon walnuts), you'll derive greatest dividends from the pies: chocolate cream, butterscotch cream, lemon icebox and the half-a-foot-high chocolate turtle ice cream pie. If you happen to overindulge, the restrooms are thoughtfully equipped with an Etch-a-Sketch and a Barbie Shopping Spree game to help you pass the time.

ALECK'S BARBECUE HEAVEN

BARBECUE

783 MARTIN LUTHER KING JR. DRIVE
DOWNTOWN
404-525-2062
11A-10P MON-WED
11A-11P THU
11A-1A FRI-SAT
1-8P SUN
NO PLASTIC

From the ill-fitting screen door that announces your arrival with a resounding slap to the well-stoked pit up front containing racks of ribs basted with their mind-blowing Come Back sauce, everything about this place rings genuine. Rib worshipers from across Atlanta flock to the smoky chapel that is Aleck's, and most of them know without being told that if the three tables are full, you stand there patiently—you don't plop yourself down in the solitary booth dedicated to Martin Luther King.

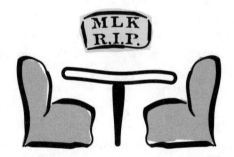

While waiting for a seat, you can enjoy the subtle artistry required for stripping ribs of their meat and deftly hacking it into bite-sized hunks for sandwiches. The tools of the trade are a cleaver and a gigantic butcher block pounded concave as a calypso drum over the years, and most days Sporty is the man putting on the show. The somewhat unorthodox sandwiches (about $5) are superb, and recommended for less ambitious appetites. They are also a better choice for excessively fastidious souls; otherwise, get your ticket punched for a rack of ribs (about $8-$10) with a stack of white bread for soaking up whatever sauce fails to find its way into your mouth or onto your clothing.

If you feel compelled to order chicken—very good, mind you, but hardly the reason to come here—then so be it, but for god's sake don't let them catch you using a knife and fork. That sort of prissiness carries no truck in these parts, so unless you want to be reprimanded loudly enough to take everyone's mind off the *Hunter* rerun that's usually cranked during lunch, you'll roll up them sleeves, grab a pile of napkins, and get busy.

> *I DROVE FOR ABOUT FIFTEEN MINUTES BEFORE I SAW A CLEAN OPEN BARBEQUE JOINT. I CAME OUT WITH TWO BIRDS. PEACHES MIGHT BE REALLY HUNGRY FOR BARBEQUED CHICKEN. IT MADE SOLID SENSE TO BROWN-NOSE MISS PEACHES.*
>
> Iceberg Slim
> Pimp (1969)

AMERICAN ROADHOUSE
ECLECTIC SOUTHERN

From esoteric regional specialties to a traditional turkey with stuffing, this place delivers a homey alternative to bar food that'll have you letting your belt out a notch or two and jonesing for a recliner. Mate this with hardwood floors, a bustling kitchen and the low-level din of rock and roll, and you have a sort of neo-juke-joint (albeit a somewhat sanitized interpretation) that proves quite inviting.

Breakfast is a strong suit, to be sure, and served any time: aside from the hearty omelets

842 NORTH
HIGHLAND AVE.
VIRGINIA-HIGHLANDS
404-872-2822
7A-11P MON-THU
7A-12A FRI-SUN
V/MC/AMEX

(served with home fries or fruit, toast or bagel), they offer up pancakes, French toast and waffles in a delicious variety for around $5. Their version of a smoothie (bananas, strawberries, vanilla yogurt, wheat germ, and protein powder) rates serious consideration for the health-obsessed. Plate lunch specials, served with two vegetables and a pair of nifty corn muffins topped with toasted pecans, are rarely less than memorable. Besides the aforementioned turkey, other solid options include the meatloaf and the basil-tinged salmon. The vegetable sheet usually runs to about 15 choices, and displays the Roadhouse kitchen crew's reverence for the traditional (sweet potatoes, locally grown collard greens), as well as their flair for the eclectic (garlic-tinged mashed potatoes, spicy five-pepper broccoli, even marinated artichoke hearts).

Come dinnertime, you can get started with a mound of chili fries, a basketful of hot wings, or, for something slightly swankier, their homemade, thick-sliced potato chips with blue cheese. If you're in a salad mood look hard at the caesar, either straight-up or with a topper of grilled chicken ($4-$6). Pasta dishes (served with garlic bread) are a pile of food for the money; especially memorable is the Pasta New Orleans, with blackened chicken and andouille sausage in a cream sauce.

Since by this point any immediate concerns regarding caloric intake have probably have been tossed aside like last week's nicotine patch, get one of their absurdly thick milkshakes or a Black Cow (vanilla ice cream in a root beer bath). On your way out, give a salute to the giant, wall-mounted American flag and grab a complimentary piece of Bazooka Joe bubble gum.

ATHENS PIZZA
PIZZA

Once the carefully guarded secret of Atlanta's sizeable Greek community as well as Emory students and faculty, Athens has in recent years blossomed into a successful local chain (their latest expansion resulted in a string of Athens Express delivery-only outlets). If this sounds like a familiar recipe for a nosedive in quality, rest easy; for now, anyway, they continue to crank out consistently fine pizzas and gyros while maintaining an unaffected, come-as-you-are atmosphere that attracts everyone from young families to beer-guzzling softball teams.

The pizza pies are relatively thin with a moderately crispy crust; with a couple of toppings, they'll set you back about $10-$12 for a medium, maybe $15 or so for a large. A favorite topping is that dairy equivalent of the anchovy, feta cheese, which adds a pleasantly strong, salty flavor. Beyond that, you'll find the usual litany of doodads: pepperoni, sausage, onions, mushrooms, green or black olives, and so on. The pasta dishes are filling and then some, characterized by a snappy red sauce and served with a basket of toasted bread and a small Greek salad.

In more of a Mediterranean vein, the gyro platter makes a fine choice. It's served with a mound of meat—that spicy, vertically cooked lamb and beef composite—a grilled pita, onions, lettuce and spicy, skin-on potatoes for around $5. Other solid bets lurking within the menu include the flaky

5550 PEACHTREE
INDUSTRIAL ROAD
CHAMBLEE
770-452-8282

1565 HIGHWAY 138
CONYERS
770-483-6228

1341 CLAIRMONT ROAD
DECATUR
404-636-1100

1255 JOHNSON
FERRY ROAD
MARIETTA
770-509-0099

11235 ALPHARETTA HWY.
ROSWELL
770-751-6629

11A-10P SUN-MON
11A-11P TUES-SAT
V/MC/AMEX

spanakopita (spinach turnovers) and the pastichio (a Greekified lasagna). For dessert, they put out a strong baklava (layer upon layer of parchment-thin fillo dough dredged with walnuts and honey) and coulemadas (a dry cookie dusted with powdered sugar—try it with a cup of their powerful coffee).

BABY JANE'S BISCUITS
BISCUITS & BREAKFAST

1052 NORTHSIDE DRIVE
NW ATLANTA
404-873-1785
6A-3P MON-FRI
7A-1P SAT
NO PLASTIC

Regulars gravitate to the odd charm of Baby Jane's' don't-mind-the-duct-tape furnishings as much as they do the righteous Southern eats. Only adding to the allure are the prices, so suspiciously low you can hardly help but wonder if the place is a front for a diamond fencing operation or something. Don't ask, don't tell—ain't that the way the big boys play it?

It should come as no surprise that the specialty of this house is amazingly light biscuits; it is somewhat less predictable that they're prepared by a sweet Korean lady named Soo, who rises well in advance of the sun to start cranking out hearty breakfasts by 6 a.m. Aside from the biscuits, you can treat yourself to a sizeable sit-down morning meal for under $3, with an array of pancakes, grits, sausage, and so on. Everything is served in a flash so you can get to your seat, finish your meal and a second cup of coffee, and still have a few minutes to eyeball the paper.

Come lunchtime, there are typically two or three meats on offer—the country-fried steak is good enough, but definitely second fiddle to the excellent fried chicken—along with six or seven vegetables, of which the pinto beans and pleasantly lumpy mashed potatoes are particular standouts. A plate inclusive of meat, two veggies, tea, and two breads can be had for under $5. Resist the temptation to get two biscuits and try one of the corn muffins, which are crunchy and fairly sweet.

The stretch of Northside Drive that Baby Jane's calls home has a decidedly industrial je ne sais quoi; as with many small restaurants of consequence, it attracts regulars from across the spectrum, particularly those ballsy enough to whip into the tiny parking lot and demand a space. Were one to generalize, however, it would be safe to say that much of the clientele is from the Love-It-or-Leave-It school; this, in combination with Soo's accommodating nature, can result in your getting an earful of Rush Limbaugh during the lunch hours.

THY MORNING BOUNTIES ERE I LEFT MY HOME,

THE BISCUIT, OR CONFECTIONARY PLUM

William Cowper
On the Receipt of My
Mother's Picture (1790)

BAGEL PALACE
DELI AND BAKERY
BAGELS

Despite a sizeable Jewish population, Atlanta—like every other Southern city with the possible exception of Miami— has never been known for its delis. Why this is remains unclear, but at any rate the Palace stands Gibraltar-like in a sea of fatty corned beef and half-assed bagels. Once you get past the shopping plaza exterior, it's like stepping into a Brooklyn neighborhood deli, complete with 20-plus cream cheese variations and occasionally surly service. With two large dining areas, it's only during the brunch rush that you may have to wait for a table. Expect to wait

2869 N. DRUID HILLS
ROAD
404-315-9016
404-315-9017
7A-7P MON-SAT
7A-4P SUN
V/MC

as long as 10 minutes, however, if you're getting bagels to-go, as they are brokered at a counter separate from the cream-cheese-and-lox area.

Breakfasts here are tremendous and frenetic, especially on the weekends. The superior pancakes and poofy French toast made with challah (a braided egg bread) will leave you wondering—that is, if you aren't already—why sober people ever go to IHOP. For those with a taste for smoked fish, a well-stocked platter of lox costs $7.50 or so and includes a cream cheese bagel, tomato, lettuce, onions, cucumbers, and olives. Other worthwhile orders are the pancake-like potato latkes (served with sour cream or apple sauce) and the cheese blintzes with sour cream and fruit preserves, both at around $3 a pop. They also offer knishes (potato or spinach for best results), heavy-duty dumplings not often done justice outside the Big Apple. Too many of these can leave you a little thick through the ankles, but my lord are they fine.

Lunch and dinner bring a wide selection of sandwiches, highlighted by a hefty Reuben, a delightful whitefish salad, and a positively bitchin' open-faced brisket with gravy (sided with fries and cole slaw). For these, figure on dropping $4-$6; as an alternative, consider half a sandwich and a bowl of their chicken soup with matzoh balls (so powerful it's been reported to shrink tumors), or two large knockwursts with baked beans, kraut and bread. If you've got any crumb-crushers in your party, the kid's menu offers full meals for under $3, including a drink and a cookie.

SAFETY EXPERTS AGREE THAT IT IS NECESSARY TO WAIT A WEEK BEFORE GOING INTO THE WATER AFTER EATING A HOT KNISH.

Tom Buckley
in the New York Times
(1976)

BARBECUE KITCHEN
MEAT-&-THREE
BARBECUE

Seasoned travelers in this region come to know Hartsfield International intimately, and they also quickly come to know its attendant dining perils. Shining like a light amid the surrounding vortex of ragtag motels and fast food eateries is R. C. Yarbrough's Barbecue Kitchen, which has ranked among the Southside's most reliable dining houses since the late sixties. By turning out very good meat-and-three plate lunches in addition to the tender and smoky barbecue, they provide a one-two that, particularly given the competition, is nigh on irresistible.

Its proximity to the airport means that, depending on the shift schedule of baggage handlers and ticket agents, you may find the cavernous dining rooms either packed or strangely desolate. Regardless, the turnover is fairly rapid and there's rarely a serious wait. Once seated, you can choose with confidence from either the chopped pork or any of the chicken alternatives—smoked or fried are especially fulfilling. The side dish list usually runs to about eight or so, and second helpings are on the house; you can't go wrong with the solid cornbread dressing, baked squash or green beans simmered with hamhocks, but steer clear of the bland mashed potatoes and gravy and the rather medicinal-tasting cole slaw.

Breadwise, opt for either the slightly salty biscuits or the crumbly, pleasantly sweet cornbread over the quite ordinary yeast rolls. For dessert, treat

1437 Virginia Ave.
College Park
404-766-9906
7a-10:30p Daily
No plastic

Going to a white-run barbeque is, I think, like going to a gentile internist: It might turn out all right, but you haven't made any attempt to take advantage of the percentages.

Calvin Trillin
(1935 -)

yourself to a bowl of memorable rice or banana pudding, or perhaps strawberry or peach cobbler. If you enjoy that singularly Southern treat boiled peanuts, grab a freshly packed bag of 'em on your way out. Visitors from other parts of the country (and beyond) will likely find these slippery legumes at least as interesting—culturally speaking—as that revered and perhaps overly razzed breakfast starch known as grits.

THE BASKET BAKERY
BAKED GOODS
GERMAN

6655 MEMORIAL DRIVE
STONE MOUNTAIN
VILLAGE
770-498-0329
7A-9P TUE-THU
7A-10P FRI-SAT
11A-4P SUN
V/MC/AMEX

Located near Stone Mountain Park's west gate, the Basket Bakery's cuisine, like Marlene Dietrich, has a heavy German accent. While the menu is chock full of hearty Bavarian delights, though, common is the patron who comes here daily and never notices. They roll in hellbent on nothing more than the legendary baked goods: pastries, croissants and bread cooked in massive stone hearth ovens, the aroma filling the entire neighborhood like the olfactory equivalent of a siren's song.

Regardless of the hour, hearty breakfasts abound with eggs, sausages, potatoes and their amazing fresh bread, which comes sided with butter and homemade jam. After a visit or two you'll likely experience deep misgivings as regards the American notion of pre-packaged, pre-sliced bread, drawn inexorably to the wisdom of the European tradition of buying a fresh loaf every time a newspaper hits your stoop.

For lunches in the $5 range, order up any of their large sandwiches or salads, or a slice of quiche. Though delicious, the hot lunch selections are a little on the spendy side. Dinner, on the other hand, is a terrific bargain (mostly in $6-$9 territory). In addition to varying specials, they come across with a permanent assortment of German dishes titillating enough to keep Colonel Klink's monocle fogged well into the night. Wonderful things like greyrer spatzle (a soft noodle they make on site, served with sauteed onions and capped with Swiss cheese); Vienna schnitzel (lightly fried veal medallions served with a vegetable and warm potato salad); and a plate featuring two large bratwursts laid up on a bed of apple-laced sauerkraut, with parsley potatoes on the side. If the weather is nice, snag a seat out on the deck-cum-beer garden and sip on a German ale.

*THE SMELL OF BUT-
TERED TOAST SIMPLY
TALKED TO TOAD, AND
WITH NO UNCERTAIN
VOICE; TALKED OF
WARM KITCHENS, OF
BREAKFASTS ON
BRIGHT FROSTY
MORNINGS . . .*

Kenneth Grahame
The Wind in the
Willows (1908)

THE BEAUTIFUL RESTAURANT
SOUL FOOD

Just getting to The Beautiful Restaurant—a hop and a skip from the Martin Luther King Center for Nonviolent Social Change and across the street from Ebenezer Baptist Church—can provide you with the niftiest dose of history this side of a Ken Burns film. And if you haven't done so already, a visit to any of these three landmarks in the neighborhood known as Sweet Auburn will stir powerful, though not necessarily similar, emotions.

While the wood panelling and naugahyde booths are showing signs of age, the cafeteria-style steam table works as well as it ever did, and you'll

397 AUBURN AVE.
DOWNTOWN
404-223-0080

2260 CASCADE ROAD SW
SW ATLANTA
404-752-5931

7A-8:30P MON-SAT
11A-8:30P SUN
NO PLASTIC

likely find it brimming with enough eye-catching items that you could give a damn about upholstery. Come by during the morning hours, and you'll find breakfast to be a solid bargain no matter how you configure it; for under three bills you can sit down to a mess of bacon, eggs, grits and toast, and $1.50 gets you a nifty bacon and egg sandwich. There are also several perpetual specials, like buttermilk pancakes by the everloving stack or grilled salmon, each served with eggs and potatoes.

For lunch and dinner you make your way along a cafeteria line, passing as you go a half-dozen each in the way of meats and hot vegetables. The barbecued beef ribs bathed in sauce are tender and meaty, the simmered chicken wings a pleasant surprise; for the dedicated gnawers in your group, oxtails and pork neck bones also make regular appearances.

The sides are generally a strong suit, and whatever you do don't leave without trying the collard greens and the baked yellow squash. Cornbread is done up in little loaves that tend in the direction of dryness, so if it comes down to a choice consider reserving the belly room for a dish of banana pudding the way it was meant to be: thick with sliced fruit and topped with sweaty meringue and vanilla wafers. The small is a buck; the large is advised only for those diners who have received clearance from a physician.

BENNY'S BARBECUE

BARBECUE

Most everyone has heard (if not cracked) the tired jokes about cops and donuts, but tailing a squad car down here below the Mason-Dixon is more likely to lead you to a barbecue pit than to a rack of maple-iced crullers. Benny's is a favorite stop among the po-lice, such that on days when the criminal types are taking a break the parking lot can resemble a casting call for *Smokey and the Bandit, Part IV*.

Situated in a dumpy little strip center—that narrows it down, doesn't it?—at the intersection of Ashford Dunwoody and Johnson Ferry roads (just south of Perimeter Mall), Benny's porcine vittles are done up with a loving hand. Not that the other offerings (chicken, beef, or turkey) aren't worth a gander, but everyone from the square-jawed sergeant to the supple-wristed purse-snatcher seems to find the pork unbeatable. For best results, order your meat with a mix of their two sauces (i.e., half hot, half not) and don't miss the potato salad, baked beans, marinated slaw and Brunswick stew, all of which, to use the rapper's parlance, rock the house. All menu items are available for takeout and Benny also does a sizeable catering trade, his primary customers being the throngs of corporate folk holed up in hermetically sealed offices surrounding Perimeter Mall.

If a bargain is your main concern, the $4.75 lunch special is served from 11 o'clock clear up until 4 in the afternoon, Monday through Saturday; it includes a sandwich, two sides and a drink.

2150-B JOHNSON FERRY ROAD
BROOKHAVEN
770-454-7810
11A-9:30P MON-SAT
NO PLASTIC

WHAT CHOWDER IS IN THE NORTH, A GUMBO IS TO THE PEOPLE OF THE FAR SOUTHERN STATES, A BRUNSWICK STEW TO VIRGINIANS, A TERRAPIN TO MARY-LANDERS, AND A BURGOO TO KENTUCKIANS.

The Boston-Cooking School Magazine (1907)

By contrast, should maximum volume be your raison d'etre, dinner platters (including bread and two sides) range from a shade under $7 to an enormous $11.55 three-meat combo, which may have you appreciating the fact that the heart specialists at St. Joseph's Hospital are so close at hand.

BIG ED'S
PIG 'N PIT
BARBECUE

1410 TERRELL
MILL ROAD
MARIETTA
770-952-9841
10:30A-9P MON-SAT
NO PLASTIC

Nowhere in the Atlanta area will you find a higher concentration of reputable barbecue houses than in Marietta. And while it may not have the history of some of it's nearby competitors, Big Ed's—which, much like Atlanta itself, rose phoenix-like from the ashes of a fire that levelled the place a few years back—has made quite a name for itself in recent years by turning out consistently strong pork-laden meals.

If you've got anything resembling a real appetite at midday, you'll want to queue up for the $5.95 all-you-can-eat lunch, which, in addition to barbecue (obviously), comes with a cast of accouterments: Brunswick stew, french fries, baked beans, a pillow of that crazy Texas toast and iced tea. Meatwise, pulled pork rules the roost, especially when paired with a little of their brick red barbecue sauce on the side. The initial portion is large enough that a request for seconds is liable to elicit a faintly disdainful "you wanna reorder?" from the girl at the counter.

If it's lighter fare you're after, opt for the $4.95 barbecue salad, which is a good pile of tender 'cue atop chopped iceberg lettuce. Fancy it ain't, but the marriage is a surprisingly happy one.

The post-blaze Ed's is bigger than the original, and the neo-roadhouse look they've adopted is pleasant enough, though the unpadded wooden booths can be hard enough on your caboose to discourage lengthy after-dinner conversations. By way of entertainment, nothing beats watching Ed run the show during the lunch rush. To see the man in action—seemingly at once he can take a 20-person order at the drive-through, delegate someone to restock the corn-on-the-cob, and stir the vat of sweet tea with his specially designed broomstick—is to have some idea what it was to witness a great field general like Robert E. Lee marshalling his troops with flawless efficiency.

You can't reach the pinnacle of true barbecue without hardwood smoke, a slow fire, and time, precious time. No matter how you cut it, slice it, chop it, or pull it, you can't make real barbecue in a hurry.

John Egerton
in Southern Living
(1990)

Big Greg's Barbecue

BARBECUE

1479 Scott Blvd.
Decatur
404-378-6041
7:30a-3:30p Sun-Tue
7a-9:30p Wed-Sat
V/MC

Like his fictional (and considerably slower witted) counterpart Forrest Gump, Big Greg Staffins has found his true calling as a feeder of the masses (albeit pork instead of shrimp) after a circuitous life that has included college football (he played on the University of Georgia's 1980 national championship team) and service to his country (sort of—he's the governor-appointed chairman of a state small business advisory committee). Alas, had Hollywood seized on the tale of our hero instead of Gump, Greg's trademark phrase might have been, "Life is like a bowl of Brunswick stew."

After years of catering political events, Staffins opened Big Greg's, a sort of barbecue pit/meat-and-three hybrid that manages the unlikely feat of delivering both with aplomb. Items of maximum interest include top-notch barbecued pork, beef and chicken, along with an admirable asssortment of vegetables and other hearty side dishes (the pinto beans, turnip greens, fried okra and sweet potato souffle all rank in the upper percentiles). At lunch, the pork sandwich is a true can't-miss proposition; if you crave something a little more well-rounded, a fiver buys you one of the four daily entree specials (country-fried steak, baked chicken and dressing, beef tips on rice, and meatloaf are regulars in the rotation) along with two vegetables.

A sliced meat platter (pork is $8, beef and chicken more like $9) might be a better idea for big dinner appetites. Contrary to the usual pattern, ribs are actually cheaper here ($7 for a modest basket, with fries), and other inexpensive options include the outstanding homemade chicken pot pie ($5). In addition to the midday and evening meat throwdowns, they also take breakfast pretty seriously at Big Greg's, offering a big spread daily that includes most of the morning meal staples (read: eggs and meat) favored by Americans, as well as their immensely popular strawberry pancakes.

BOBBY AND JUNE'S KOUNTRY KITCHEN

MEAT-&-THREE

With its log cabin facade looking marvelously out of place among the prosthetic supply houses and automotive repair shops along 14th Street, Bobby and June's boasts some of the best biscuits in town, not to mention a dining room decorated with enough farm implements so as to risk being mistaken for a *Green Acres* retrospective.

Breakfast is played pretty close to the traditional vest, highlighted by hotcakes and all the endearingly salty meats you could hope for. Later in the day, meat-and-three plate lunches are the thing (generally $6 or less), with the gravy-covered country-fried steak and tender barbecued pork stealing the spotlight. The fried chicken, be forewarned, often suffers from an unfortunate dryness. As a group, the veggies are credibly rendered if something short of a revelation, with the delicate fried okra (a notoriously difficult-to-master Southern treat) a surprising highlight. Whenever you drop in, whatever you order, make sure everyone gets a couple of those righteous biscuits or you could wind up with a fistfight on your hands.

The busy lunch crowd is handled efficiently by the somewhat acerbic Bobby, who implores you to wait in a little entry hall a table clears, then barks a command for you to take a seat. It can seem a tad harrowing to the uninitiated, but once seated you get to enjoy your lunch while the rest of the patrons undergo a similar hazing. Pay on your way out, and check out the giant coloring books they sell at the register. Sayeth June: "Kids love 'em!"

375 14TH STREET
MIDTOWN
404-876-3872
6A-8P MON-FRI
6A-2P SAT
V/MC/AMEX

IT IS TIME TO EAT. HERE IS SUPPER. BLACK-EYED PEAS WITH HAM HOCK ... FRIED OKRA ... COUNTRY CORN BREAD ... SWEET POTATO PIE ... YOU TALK OF SUPPING WITH THE GODS. YOU'VE JUST DONE IT, FOR WHO BUT A GOD COULD HAVE COME UP WITH THE DIVINE FACT OF OKRA?

James Dickey (1923 -)

BRIDGETOWN GRILL
CARIBBEAN

1156 EUCLID AVE.
LITTLE FIVE POINTS
404-653-0110

689 PEACHTREE ST.
MIDTOWN
404-873-5361

11:30A-10:30P
SUN-THU
11:30A-11P FRI-SAT
V/MC/AMEX

RUB AN OLD WOMAN'S
BACK, AND SHE WILL
LET YOU TASTE HER
PEPPER POT.

Jamaican proverb

While the surgical-glove-wearing cooks at the Bridgetown draw from a variety of culinary influences, there's never any doubt that this place is forever Jamaican at heart. From the non-stop reggae lilt to the dreadlocked cashier to the picture-postcard of Bob Marley sucking a lungful from a four-inch doober, this groovy diner is a magnet for displaced Rastas and well-pierced suburban wannabes. The resulting scene, particularly in the case of the Five Points location, is rarely less than interesting.

You can either take a seat at the counter or hit the narrow strip of pink and orange booths—curiously coordinated with the waitresses outfits (and, on occasion, their hair). An order of Our Daily Bread ($1.35)—a domed pineapple egg brioche with homemade guava butter—should be requested as soon as your hiney hits the vinyl. The Nacho Mama ($5.50), bowls of black bean and beef chili, jack cheese, jalapenos, sour cream and salsa, is another nice way to start. Beyond that, a visit to the Grill should include either an order of jerk chicken or glazed pork chops. Where most places use a sauce when going the jerk route, Bridgetown employs a dry spice rub on their chicken. It's then grilled, and the end result is redolent with cumin, ginger and much red pepper. This also appears as a sandwich and in a couple of salads, including the Bridgetown Caesar ($6.25). The outstanding chops, meanwhile, are coated with a post-grilling apricot tarragon glaze. They come with black beans and rice and a salad of marinated cucumber, tomato and red onion.

The Jamaican Burritos and Tex-Jam Plate (both about $6) are fine examples of Bridgetown's occasional mix of Mexican and Jamaican influences. The latter features a chimale: a traditional corn and ham tamale topped with black bean chili and coated with jack cheese. The two best dinner-only options are the Guava BBQ Ribs (a half rack is plenty); and the Chicken and Rib Combo (a half rack and a breast of either jerk or Cuban chicken for $13.50). Exercise caution in the vicinity of Asian-sounding dishes, particularly those with the peanut-laded teriyaki sauces.

BROOKHAVEN CAFE
SEMI-VEGETARIAN

On the whole, restaurants situated inside health food stores have a nagging tendency toward culinary priggishiness, not to mention skimpy portions. The comfortable and inviting Brookhaven is one of the minority that manages to attract a broad spectrum of customers, not just the usual crowd of legume-worshippers and crystal-rubbers. Such is the popularity of this little bistro, tucked inside the goofily named Nuts and Berries, that there's often nary a seat to be had indoors or on the tiny patio; not coincidentally, the takeout trade is brisk.

Daily specials such as stir-fried vegetables over rice or a soft flour tortilla filled with hummus and

4272 PEACHTREE ROAD
(INSIDE NUTS AND BERRIES)
BROOKHAVEN
404-231-5907
11A-3:30P MON-FRI
9A-3P SAT
9A-2P SUN
NO PLASTIC

veggies are strong choices, as are the soups du jour—the bean version is nothing short of dynamite. The most consistently agreeable options, however, are from the under-$4 Mexican menu: the bean burrito (huge pintos, lowfat cheddar, sour cream, lettuce and homemade salsa) and the vegetarian chili, spooned over corn chips along with olives and cheese.

The garden burger (their own recipe) is a satisfying meatless patty on a whole wheat roll with a Dijon mustard so caustic it's like one notch shy of turpentine. Also, there's a nice selection of sandwiches and salads for under five bucks, including a pita bulging with hot veggies, a green salad with grilled chicken, and a tuna melt with more of that ubiquitous lowfat cheese. Most everything comes with tortilla chips or carrot sticks.

For fanatical granola munchers, most menu items are tagged with either a teeny picture of a broccoli stalk (indicating less than 10% of calories from fat) or a carrot (less than 30%). Yeah, whatever. Appetizers of note are a yummy hummus with pita wedges, salsa and chips, and a racy bean dip (also with chips). The baked desserts are uniformly dry and unexciting; if you want something sweet, instead try one of the bodacious $2 fruit smoothies, made with blueberries, bananas, apples, strawberries and whatever other organica they have lying around.

BUCKHEAD DINER
ECLECTIC AMERICAN

While there are dozens of Atlanta restaurants with inflated reputations, more than a few deliver more seem to be in some covert competition to determine who can deliver the least food on the largest plates for the most money. In the case of the ridiculously popular Buckhead Diner, the hoo-hah is by and large justified. With beautifully prepared chow (in hair-raisingly large portions) and a crack waitstaff, it remains a solid dining value if not exactly the cheapest place to tie on a feedbag.

The ostentatious shiny metal exterior is an attention grabber to be sure, but it's probably the only "diner" featuring valet parkers and a bar dispensing regular shots of Chivas on the rocks. The deceptively large main dining room is surrounded by windows allowing plenty of sunlight by day and a clear view of Buckhead nightlife. The interior is designed to resemble a fancy dining car from the glory days of rail travel: dark wood trim and highly polished metal accents, deep green carpet and white linen tablecloths. The other end of the restaurant features an open kitchen (complete with dramatic flashes of fire and steam) with some counter seating, a row of two-person booths and the aformentioned bar.

The menu runs from quasi-diner fare like the Knife & Fork Chili Dog ($5.50) all the way up to the day's fresh catch (in the $15 range). Some of the swingingest appetizers ($5-$6) are the shrimp and pork spring rolls, the steamed butter clams, and the baby back ribs glazed with tamarind and

3073 PIEDMONT ROAD
BUCKHEAD
404-262-3336
11A-12A MON-SAT
10A-10P SUN
V/MC/AMEX

served with fried plantains and black bean mango salsa. The roster of sandwiches is also impressive: try the nearly decadent open-faced, grilled salmon BLT on potato/dill bread, or the towering cheeseburgers (a mere half pound) on poppy seed rolls with grilled red onions. All are served with a mound of homemade, thick-sliced potato chips.

The smoked pork chop (served with spinach, cheese grits and warm black-eyed pea salsa) tends to cause a clamor, and it's so absurdly huge that cartoon lovers compare it to the slab that tipped the Flinstone's vehicle sideways. The veal-and-wild-mushroom meatloaf with a side of celery/fried onion mashed potatoes also hits the spot ($11.50). By this point, the very thought of dessert may be enough to have you getting Dr. Kevorkian on the horn; but if you're still good to go, bear down on either the towering, spongy peach bread pudding (on a plateful of Southern Comfort cream, for the love of Mike), or the crusty, buttery upside-down apple pie topped with cinnamon ice cream.

CAFE DIEM
COFFEEHOUSE

640 NORTH HIGHLAND
AVE.
PONCEY-HIGHLANDS
11:30A-12A MON-THU
11:30A-2A FRI
11A-2A SAT
11A-12A SUN
404-607-7008
V/MC/AMEX

Creviced between a transient hotel and a condom store, this elder staesman among Atlanta's coffeehouses is blessed with a very limited number of nearby parking spaces—on a nightly basis, the surrounding lots see more tow truck action than a demolition derby. While this seems to be a frequent topic of conversation, the array of fancy javas, fine desserts and inexpensive sandwiches and salads are far more worthy of discussion.

Whether you stop by for an early dinner or a post-meal caffeine boost, try and grab a seat on the covered patio if the weather is at all cooperative. Failing that, you'll find the interior characterized by a high ceiling, hardwood floors and large paintings by local artists. There's also a refrigerated dessert case awaiting your inspection (take particular note of the chocolate truffle cake and the great Napoleons), and you can of course watch the expert milk frothers working their magic.

IF YOU CAN MAKE A GOOD CUP OF COFFEE, YOU CAN MAKE ANY MAN GLAD HE HAS LEFT HIS MOTHER.

Mrs. W.T. Hayes
Kentucky Cook Book
(1912)

As is customary these days, there are upwards of two dozen coffees on offer, as well as a goodly selection of teas both herbal and caffeinated. Javawise, prices range from $1.50 for a snatch of hi-test espresso to a double-shot cafe au lait (steamed milk on the side) for twice that. An individual pot (about two cups) of the coffee of the day runs $1.25. Most everything is available decaf, iced, lowfat—whatever you want.

Sandwiches (around $5) are served on crusty baguettes and served with fresh fruit and potato salad (with dill to burn). Among the best are the Diem Combo (ham, turkey, provolone, vinaigrette), the meatless veggie/grain burger, and the Mediterranean (montrachet cheese, roasted red peppers, sun-dried tomatoes, and marinated mushrooms, olives and red onions). The caesar salad topped with grilled chicken is also worth a look. And if you've had it up to here with coffee, try a fresh-squeezed carrot-apple juice to wash it all down.

CAJUN KITCHEN

CAJUN

842 MARIETTA ST.
(INSIDE THE SOMBER
REPTILE)
DOWNTOWN
404-881-9701
11A-9P MON-THU
11A-12A FRI-SAT
12P-9P SUN
NO PLASTIC

Located within a jazz and blues nightclub, the Cajun Kitchen has retained a sizeable percentage of their regulars even after the owners transformed the club from the previous incarnation as a punk/heavy metal venue. At least from a dining standpoint, it's hard not to read this metamorphosis—gone are the black interior walls, ear plug vending machine and, as far as I've seen anyway, the inevitable smashed toilets—as a positive. With a fresh coat of paint and windows that actually allow sunlight to penetrate, the Creole delights are in a considerably more compatible environment.

The area previously serving as a frenzied midnight mosh pit is these days lined with tables covered in red-and-black checkered vinyl and topped with a daunting assortment of hot pepper sauces. The daily plate lunch special runs $5.95 and is usually worth a hard look, but don't be too quick to dismiss the delicious assortment of huge poor boy sandwiches, which come with beans or fresh-cut fries. Packed with your choice of 11 fillings—most notably shrimp (get 'em grilled); oysters (get 'em fried); and catfish (just get it), they run $6 and change. Regular sandwiches are smaller and—guess what—cheaper (around $3-$4).

A few steps further from the beaten path lies the Blackened Voodoo Chicken Salad, which exudes bayou mojo the way Bill Gates gives off nerdiness. Even hearty eaters should have little trouble getting a couple of meals out of one whopping serving. Otherwise, the boudin balls (a dandy liver and

MR. PRESIDENT, PEOPLE UP IN THIS PART OF THE COUNTRY NEVER HAVE LEARNED TO FRY OYSTERS AS WELL AS WE HAVE DONE DOWN OUR WAY.

Louisiana senator Huey Long
in a filibuster oration
(1935)

rice sausage) and cayenne-laced Cajun hushpuppies are good enough to tease any palate, as are the chicken/andouille sausage gumbo and the red beans and rice—though a healthy splash of Tabasco does them no harm. Meat abstainers will find a vegetarian menu available as well.

CANTON HOUSE
CHINESE

Doraville has become something of a nexus for Atlanta's substantial Asian community, and not coincidentally it is home to some top caliber eateries. Where the subject is Chinese food—more specifically, Cantonese—you'll be hard-pressed to top the goodies cranked out at Canton House. And if you hanker especially for the array of snack-sized morsels that collectively travel under the heading "dim sum," then you need look no further.

Though offered daily at lunch, the big dim sum doings are weekend mornings, when the menu is considerably expanded. Crowds begin forming by 10 a.m., the idea being that when it comes to steamy pork-filled buns, scallion pies and delicate pastries, having first crack can mean the difference between smiling and sorry. It may sound a bit fanatical given that the two dining rooms easily seat more than 100 people, but once the food-laden carts begin their circuit you can quickly find yourself sitting shoulder-to-shoulder with strangers, peering into the stacked steel containers and hollering like an auctioneer as the servers display their wares.

To keep track of your tab they leave a ticket on your table, tacking on a few Chinese characters

4825 BUFORD HWY.
DORAVILLE
770-936-9030
11A-3P, 5P-10:30P
MON-THU
11A-3P, 5P-11P FRI
10:30A-11P SAT
10:30A-10:30P SUN
V/MC/AMEX

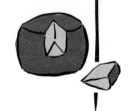

after each order (prices range from $1.70 to $5.60 for large dishes like mussels or roast duck). Unless you grew up eating this stuff you're likely to require some explanation, and not all of the dapper servers are fluent in English. Those who are will gladly fill you in, though be advised that they often have several people peppering them with questions at once.

At any rate it's hard to go wrong; the translucent, splendorous har kaw (rice-flour dumplings filled with meat), shu mei (filled with minced shrimp, pork and black mushrooms), salty sauteed oysters on the halfshell topped with black beans, and sticky rice wrapped in lotus leaves are but a few of the dozens of divine possibilities. A steady supply of steeped oolong tea keeps everything sliding down the hatch.

If you're stopping by for a weekday lunch you'll do well to order from the sizeable Cantonese menu (everything's under $6), highlighted by a stirring selection of soups and plenty of noodles. And if you say yes to a seat in the smoking section, make sure you mean it; it can often resemble a scene from *Backdraft*, with diners apt to snag ashtrays from neighboring tables as theirs' fill up. No matter where you sit you can look forward to an earful of seventies rock.

CANTONESE WILL EAT ANYTHING IN THE SKY BUT AIRPLANES, ANYTHING IN THE SEA BUT SUBMARINES, AND ANYTHING WITH FOUR LEGS BUT THE TABLE.

Amanda Bennett
in the Wall Street
Journal (1983)

CAPRI ITALIAN AMERICAN CAFE

ITALIAN

Nestled in a tiny—everybody now—strip mall a couple of miles east of I-85, the Capri isn't on the way to much of anything but it's nonetheless a worthwhile detour for a weekday lunch or dinner. Formerly known as Park Bench Cafe, the place is still owned by Aniello and Pina Vellino, a couple of talented cooks who keep the kitchen staffed primarily with family members. New shingle, same high quality eats.

Lunchtime highlights include a snazzy list of salads as well as cold or grilled sandwiches; of particular note is the Italian chicken breast, a boneless filet marinated in a supple vinaigrette and served fully dressed on a large, soft hoagie. All the hot sandwiches come with a monstrous serving of fries for under $4.50. These tend to be pretty filling, but if you're feeling especially peckish try a cup of black bean soup—brimming with sweet onions and cilantro—for a kicker.

They keep things fairly simple come the dinner hour, with hearty pasta dishes carrying the banner. Their homemade marinara sings a sweet song when ladled over fettuccine or spaghetti, and the alfredo sauce is every bit its equal. With the exception of the slightly pricier lasagna, pasta dishes (accompanied by salad and garlic bread) ring in at under $8. There are also several specialty dinners offered, like meatball parmigiana (homemade meatballs smothered in mozzarella) and the grilled Island chicken breast that's marinated in a perky

3210 TUCKER-NORCROSS ROAD
TUCKER
770-493-9317
11A- 2:30P, 5-9P
MON-FRI
NO PLASTIC

EVERYTHING YOU SEE I OWE TO SPAGHETTI.

Sophia Loren
(1934 -)

fusion of jerk-type spices—both are $10. A respectable selection of both beer and wine are on offer, as is the requisite litany of espresso beverages. Try one with a slice of cheesecake, or snag one of their homemade brownies or lemon bars for the road.

CAREY'S PLACE
BURGERS

1021 Cobb Parkway
Marietta
770-422-8042
11a-12a Mon-Sat
12p-12a Sun
No Plastic

What appears at first glance to be your garden variety honkytonk is a honkytonk, alright, but decidedly not run-of-the-mill. Aside from the politically incorrect jukebox and a collection of autographed country music photos that leaves nary a square inch of exposed wall, Carey's main distinguishing characteristic is its exceptional hamburgers.

During lunch you can battle for a table or grab a seat at the bar. After they take your order, be patient because they don't pre-prepare any of their food. For that reason, too arrive either famished or in a hurry is to invite frustration. You can pass the time by pumping quarters into the sawdust-covered bowling machine or check out the telly—chances are good it'll be tuned to one of those body-shaping show on ESPN.

According to Carey's son, Jay, the secret to the burgers lies in their seasoning. The half-pound, saucer-sized patties are spiked with a homemade spice recipe (more than a hint of garlic powder and oregano) of which they are quite proud and protective. These units are grilled to order and loaded with lettuce, tomato, onion and real mayo—the result is nothing short of spectacular. Burgers aside, they also serve a tasty grilled chicken sand-

It requires a certain type of mind to see the beauty in a hamburger bun. Yet, is it any more unusual to find grace in the curved silhouette of a bun . . . than in the arrangement of textures and colors in a butterfly's wing?

Ray Kroc
Grinding It Out (1977)

wich, Polish sausages and a somewhat pricey ribeye. All meals come with an order of thick-cut fries. As to the beverage question, go for an icy glass of Schweppe's ginger ale, served draft style. And, in addition to the wall of mug shots, you stand a pretty fair chance of spotting a star or two in the flesh (Marietta native Travis Tritt signed his Warner Brothers record contract here).

CASABLANCA
CUBAN & SPANISH

Although this place was for the past few years known as The Spanish Cafe, it recently changed hands and reopened as Casablanca. While the menu remains much as it was under the previous administration, the quality of the grub has taken a quantum leap even as the prices have been trimmed (five bucks goes a long way). Should that rousing combination of circumstances continue, it could be the beginning of, ahem, a beautiful friendship.

4847 PEACHTREE INDUSTRIAL BLVD. CHAMBLEE 770-454-1192 11A-10P DAILY V/MC

Lunch plates are served with a choice of white or yellow rice and a cup of black bean soup, which Cubans seem to consume like Americans eat corn flakes. The soup is stocked with chunks of onion and is tasty, though it can be a shade on the salty side. Among the meat entrees, greatest rewards are to reaped by opting for the chicken or marinated pork dishes. Particular points of interest include the puerco asado (roast pork served with grilled onions) and the sensational pollo frito (a heavily herbed, pan-fried chicken). The beef items are certainly passable, but be aware that dishes like picadillo (akin to ground beef lasagna sans noodles) and the traditional favorite ropa vieja (literally, "old clothes") have a pronounced vinegar tang that some folks may find overpowering. One of the house specialties is the Pregnant Potato, a monstrous baker stuffed with ground beef and a couple of cheeses. While ordering it aloud may cause you to wince with embarassment, it's the one item containing beef that's downright worthwhile. All meals are served with a basket of buttery, lightly toasted Cuban bread.

For dinner, expect to feast on portions marginally heftier than those at lunch. When shopping for a first course, be advised that the appetizer menu is lousy with heavy dishes more apt to dull your tastebuds than sharpen them. Most any of Casablanca's terrific soups rate an infinitely better bet; best of the bowls are the garbanzo bean (chick peas, potatoes, ham and Spanish sausage), the Spanish-inspired chicken and vegetable brew, and the positively wicked caldo gallego (collard green broth stocked with navy beans, potatoes and ham).

Alcoholic beverages aren't an option, but you can get a variety of sodas and coffees (including espresso and cafe con leche). Save your hooch money for a slab of flan. As for the ambience, it's punctuated by an assortment of bullfighting posters and the energetic, folk-tinged lilt of the Gipsy Kings. A tiny back room with four booths is reserved for that segment of the population prone to lighting up at mealtime.

CLEVE'S
MEAT-&-THREE

Located just off Buford Highway, Cleve's is an oasis of Southern cooking amid some of the best Asian and Mexican restaurants in Atlanta. While the neighborhood has witnessed a rather pronounced transition from turnip greens to green cards, Cleve's has managed to hold its own with a rock-solid menu of meat-and-three offerings and a unique method of pressure-frying chicken.

The entrees are consistently good, if a bit inconsistently priced. Best deals include the country-fried steak, grilled hamsteak and the downright delicious meatloaf (all in the $4-$6 range). Cleve's special "broasted" chicken—a term since co-opted by half the supermarkets in the land—is moist and meaty and comes in a variety of guises, among them smothered in either a honey glaze or a ketchupy barbecue sauce. All meals include a side dish, of which the turnip greens and sweet potato souffle rate the grooviest. If you enjoy chicken livers—golly, who doesn't?—Cleve's dunks them in buttermilk batter and then deep fries the bejesus out of them. Try them with a little dish of the honey glaze used on the chicken. Good stuff.

If a full platter seems too much for you, Cleve's offers a baked ham or country steak sandwich, as well as a hand-patted burger, solid bargains all at less than $3. Fries and other side orders can be had for under a buck. You should also know that the desserts—usually tall wedges of layer cake—taste as fine as they look. Like more than a few things fitting that description, though, they're a tad pricey.

2503 CARROLL AVE.
CHAMBLEE
770-457-1110
11A-8P MON-THU
11A-3P FRI
NO PLASTIC

EVERYBODY HAS THE RIGHT TO NOMINATE WHOSE FOOD IS THE MOST GORGEOUS, AND I NOMINATE GEORGIA'S.

Ogden Nash
introduction to The Savannah Cook Book
(1933)

Coco Loco
CARIBBEAN

2625 PIEDMONT ROAD
NE ATLANTA
404-364-0212
11A-2:30P, 6-10P
MON-THU
11A-10:30P FRI
12P-11P SAT
1-9P SUN
V/MC/AMEX

*WILL IS THE PIMP OF
APPETITE.*

Lope de Vega
The Crazy People of
Valencia (c. 1600)

In a city these days teeming with solid Caribbean (especially Cuban) restaurants, Coco Loco belongs on the A-list. From their selection of terrific sandwiches to the high-end seafood offerings, they deliver quality and value without fail. And though suffering the familiar Atlanta ignominy of a strip center address (Home Depot and KFC are neighbors), the place manages to rise above its mundane surroundings, exuding no small amount of Antilles charm.

Lunches are in the $5 range, with specials changing daily. The picadillo sided with black beans and rice is one to watch for: served in a broad ceramic bowl, it's chock-a-block with lean ground beef, onions, green peppers and raisins. Half a Cuban or boliche sandwich paired with beans and rice or salad is a slightly less rib-sticking but equally tasty option. Keep your whistle wet with a chilly ginger beer or one of the Coco-Rico sodas.

When the sun goes down, things get a mite fancier. Among the finest of the fine are the chicharron de pollo (Dominican-style chicken, marinated in ginger and bitter orange juice then skillet fried); empanizado steak (seasoned and pan-fried sirloin); and the piquant and plentiful jerk shrimp (at $12.95, it represents the high-end of the price scale). Top to bottom, front to back, the menu is a model of creativity and consistency, so order with confidence. Should you wish to imbibe they offer a decent wine list, though anyone hankering for a taste of the grape ought seriously consider the fresh and fruity sangria ($2.95 a glass, $9.95 for a carafe).

Coco Loco's excellence extends to the dessert menu, so do whatever you must short of a purgative to reserve room for at least a taste. When in season, the papaya chunks with cream cheese are a thing of beauty, as is the natilla (a delicate caramel custard) and the traditional torta tres leches (three milk cake).

THE COLONNADE RESTAURANT
COMFORT FOOD

Ask just about anyone who grew up in Atlanta and they'll probably have a story about lunching at The Colonnade with their grandmother or great-aunt Gertie—she of the baggy hose and sensible shoes—in the days before Cheshire Bridge Road became fertile ground for strip clubs and rooms-by-the-hour motels. The place has been here seemingly since the days when General Sherman got careless with the matches, and, though the surrounding terrain has become decidedly more sleazy, the restaurant itself, both inside and out, remains far more reminiscent of *Driving Miss Daisy* than, say, *The Devil and Miss Jones*.

From work crews sporting hardhats to blue-haired grannies swaddled in fox stoles, the crowd gathers for a meat-and-two and a double shot of nostalgia. The place runs a wait as early as 11:30 a.m., with folks arriving for sliced roast beef and mushroom gravy, turkey and dressing, salmon croquettes with egg sauce, or one of more than 20 other comfort platters. Apart from these, there are some pricier steak and seafood dishes, but you need

1879 CHESHIRE BRIDGE ROAD
NE ATLANTA
404-874-5642
11A-2P, 5-9P MON-THU
11A-2P, 5-10P FRI-SAT
11A-9P SUN
NO PLASTIC

not trouble yourself. Baked apples, turnip greens, fried okra, and that toothsome Georgian delight, sweet potato souffle, highlight the hot vegetable list.

As for the cold selections, stay away from just about everything unless you're fond of tomato aspic or that depressing "wedge of lettuce" with French dressing—the last time that was suitable fare, *Marcus Welby, M.D.* was knocking 'em dead in the Nielsens. After finishing your third glass of iced tea, you'll do right by yourself to review the desserts. Smart money rides on the strawberry shortcake or brandy peach ice cream, particularly in summer.

Dinner is essentially a revisitation of the lunch menu, with prices jumping a dollar or two. The evening meal also finds quite a few patrons waiting for their table in the lounge, hunched over gin-and-tonics just like in the old days when people *respected* the Cocktail Hour. In a city that's a poster child for constant, damn-the-consequences change, it's nice to see a place like The Colonnade clinging to the past as though it were a beloved alligator handbag.

CRESCENT MOON
ECLECTIC AMERICAN

254 W. PONCE DE LEON AVE.
DECATUR
404-377-5623
7:30A-3P MON-FRI
8A-2P SAT
8A-2:30P SUN
V/MC

A couple of years back when the Decatur restaurant Thumb's Up got new owners and a new name, regulars held their collective breath and hoped the high-quality food and laid-back attitude would remain. Fortune smiled, thankfully, as the Altherholts—Rob and Carolyn—have crafted a culinary niche of their own with Crescent Moon, while retaining the good vibes and restraining any tendencies toward cuteness where decor is concerned.

Hearty breakfast options abound for around $5. Omeletwise, opt for the Yukon (salmon with lightly sauteed spinach and cream cheese), the Farmer's (sage sausage, potatoes, onions and cheddar cheese), or either of the two vegetable-only

choices. For something less eggy, you'll be hard-pressed to find fault with the challah (an airy Jewish egg bread) French toast; the organic whole-wheat-and-honey hotcakes; or the coarse-ground grits, griddle-fried with onions and cheddar. Weekend-only specials include a racy Tex-Mex scramble and Arnold's Eggs (grilled challah topped with two poached eggs, Canadian bacon and hollandaise). Get the picture?

For your midday repast, think salad. The grilled chicken caesar rocks, as does the fruit and cheese combo—apples, grapes, brie and blue cheese, tossed with spinach and a walnut vinaigrette. To wash it all down, $2 buys you any of their 10 freshly made fruit and vegetable juices. When the dinner bell rings, the tireless kitchen staff trots out yet another amazing menu. Appetizers of note are the chilled Oriental shrimp (marinated in ginger and teriyaki) and the

STILL SILENT, HOW-EVER, HE TOOK HIS PLACE AT THE TABLE, HIS LARGE HAIRY HANDS IDLE AND PALM-UPWARDS ON THE CLOTH. HE NEVER ATE CEREALS.

Kingsley Amis
Lucky Jim (1953)

almond-crusted chicken fingers with a peppery raspberry sauce. Saladwise, anything featuring the phrases "grilled fish" and "field greens" in the same sentence is likely to please

Entrees ($10-$13) to watch for include the creamy red-and-yellow-pepper fettuccini (with corn, tomatoes, scallions and smoked chicken); grilled rainbow trout (with snow peas, diced tomatoes and garlic, over pasta); and a smoked pork loin (drizzled with blackberry sage sauce). As if all that weren't enough, Carolyn's homemade desserts are high caliber, as are the refreshing smoothies (mango, lime and honey, or blueberry-melon).

DeKalb Farmer's Market

SANDWICHES

3000 E. Ponce De Leon Ave.
Decatur
404-377-6400
9a-9p Daily (store)
11a-8p Daily (cafe)
No Plastic

Since many of Atlanta's supermarkets have yet to be hipped to the city's increasing cultural complexity, The DeKalb Market is where quite a few of immigrants and serious chefs come to lay their hands on otherwise impossible-to-find beans, roots and fungi, not to mention live salmon, *extra* hot mango pickles and the area's best deal on fresh cut nasturtiums. With that sort of selection, it's easy to forget that there's also a little cafe cranking out freshly prepared hot food and cold salads for under $4.

Everyone from Geenlanders to Kuwaitis should feel welcomed by the huge flags representing—we'll give 'em the benefit of the doubt—every country around the globe, hanging plumb from the 40-foot ceiling. Once inside the main shopping area, the array of fresh produce is nothing short of dazzling. And that's to make no mention of the extremely comprehensive bakery, dozens of varieties of rice, live seafood and the cheapest prices on *good* beer, wines and port sherries. Van Morrison fans will even be able to pick up a commemorative jar of Tupelo honey.

If one subscribes to the old saw about it being unwise to shop when hungry, you should make a beeline for the Market Cafe. Though hardly what you'd call fancy, it's an outstanding spot to fill up on vegetables like steamed broccoli and tender yellow squash; samosas (fried dumplings loaded with ground beef, onion and peas); or beef tips in gravy over rice.

If you're concerned that the heft of a full-sized meal might adversely affect your footspeed, opt for the $3-a-pound salad bar, a bowl of beef barley soup ($2) or a sandwich. Boar's Head cold cuts (corned beef, liverwurst . . . you name it) are slathered with a strong, dark mustard and piled high on crusty baguettes, chewy Italian loaves, musky Jewish rye, and so on. When you're pinched for time, get it to go and eat while you're languishing in the inevitable lengthy check-out line.

IT IS NOT THESE WELL-FED LONG-HAIRED MEN THAT I FEAR, BUT THE PALE AND THE HUNGRY-LOOKING.

Julius Caesar
(100-44 B.C.)

Down East BBQ

BARBECUE

2289 SOUTH COBB DRIVE
SMYRNA
770-434-8887
11A-9P MON-FRI
11A-10P SAT
1P-7P SUN
NO PLASTIC

South Cobb Drive has just enough decent, small-time eateries dotting its seemingly endless stretch of chain restaurants to keep you from pulling over to the shoulder and sobbing like a rashy baby. Topping the woefully short list of places standing in the way of the whole area becoming a hellbound handbasket is Down East, one of the few purveyors of North Carolina-style barbecue you'll run across in Atlanta.

Unlike pitminders in other regions that base their sauce on tomato paste or mustard, North Carolinians prefer a vinegar-and-pepper concoction that permeates the meat, adding an interesting, some would say elegant, dimension to slow-smoked pork. Also key to the Carolina paradigm is this little culinary curveball: barbecue sandwiches are meant to be topped with cole slaw. That's the way it's done here unless you beg them to leave it off. Their's is a mild, mayo-based slaw speckled with green onion, and it mates surprisingly well with the meat. Of course, if you're feeling hesitant you can always get it on the side and experiment.

Daily lunch specials (usually some variation on a pork barbecue plate) run about $5 and include hushpuppies or cornbread (both tend to arrive a little cold, but are still sweet and tasty), slaw, and another side dish. Best of the lot are the thick and

WITHIN TEN YEARS, AS MANY PEOPLE HAVE DIED PREMATURELY IN THIS STATE (NORTH CAROLINA) FROM BAD COOKERY AS WERE SLAIN IN THE (CIVIL) WAR.

General Thomas L.
Clingman
(1875)

tangy baked beans, full of molasses and served in a styrofoam dish. Although refills are free on sodas, tea and coffee, don't be surprised if you're gently admonished by the owners for making too many trips.

THE DOWNWIND
SANDWICHES

One of the more secluded eateries in north Atlanta, the Downwind combines skillful sandwich making with an unhindered view of the north runway at DeKalb-Peachtree Airport. It's a little small inside, but there's not a bad seat in the house and if it's not too crowded you can sit on the second-story deck and check out the Cessnas taking off, as well as the occasional dirigible.

To get here, you head to the main airport entrance off Clairmont Road and wind your way to the administration building. From there you can either head up the side stairs or go through the main building entrance and walk up to the second floor. Inside you'll find a two-tiered dining area and a full bar with counter seating running along the back wall.

The decor leans unsurprisingly in the direction of an aviation theme, with everything from model Sopwith Camels to inflatable planes suspended from the ceiling. And in addition to the possibilities for observing air traffic, it's also a perfect spot for the simple pleasure of scarfing down a BLT while watching a good thunderstorm. If you arrive by land on a rainy day, though, you'd best heed the multitude of signs warning that the parking lot is prone to flash-flooding.

2000 AIRPORT ROAD
DEKALB-PEACHTREE
AIRPORT
CHAMBLEE
770-452-0973
11A-11P MON-SAT
V/MC/AMEX

ALWAYS IT WAS A CLUB SANDWICH, THE TOAST BROWN AND CRISP, THE TURKEY MOIST WITH MAYONNAISE, THE BACON SHARP AND SMOKY. . . I LOOKED OUT OVER THE BOATS ROCKING AT THEIR MOORINGS AND LAZILY WORKED MY WAY THROUGH EACH TRIANGLE. THE WAITER CALLED ME 'SIR,' THE TABLECLOTH WAS WHITE—AND I WAS VERY FOND OF SANDWICHES.

Vladimir Estragon
(1940-)

The best of the grub is the freshly roasted turkey breast sandwich on a large, soft hoagie roll with mayo and crisp lettuce. With a side of fries, it will run you about $6. For about the same money you can land a gigantic half-pound burger—topped with cheese and/or bacon, fries on the side—that's a favorite of the local flyboys. Rounding out the sandwich choices are the ham and cheese, club and BLT variety, all solid choices. Salads are also worth a try, especially the tuna (ice-cream scooped onto a bed of greens) and the Greek, with onions, tomatoes, banana peppers, olives and feta cheese.

DUNK 'N DINE
BREAKFAST

2277 CHESHIRE
BRIDGE ROAD
NE ATLANTA
404-636-0197
OPEN 24 HOURS
NO PLASTIC

With a local reputation forged through years of accommodating all manner of late-night scofflaws and bleary, morning-after malcontents, this beloved greasy spoon continues to crank out exemplary short-order meals around the clock. And although founder "Happy" Herman Mitchell no longer runs Dunk 'n Dine, the new management seems determined to maintain the diner's personality—you can, for example, still slide behind the counter and help yourself to coffee while waiting for a seat.

The breakfast offerings are about what you'd expect in a place frequented by nightowls and earlybirds and, needless to add, creativity is of little interest to most patrons. Dishes range from the How-much-change-do-I-have-in-my-ashtray fried egg sandwich to the jumbo waffle feed to the properly substantial Texas breakfast that includes three eggs, three meats(!), toast, and grits. Lunch features a number of burgers and sandwiches for under four bucks. The addition of salads to the menu is one of the few concessions to the changing times, but they generally display about as much panache as a UPS uniform. Far more satisfying supplementals include thick milkshakes, mounds of french fries doused with gravy, and slices of pecan and apple pie.

The retro setting features a long main dining area, counter seating up front (with an unhindered view of the hyperbusy grill), booths along the wall and a new al fresco patio. The latter, though nice enough, doesn't really fit the picture. There's just something reaffirming about black-and-white tile floors, formica tabletops and a thoughtfully stocked jukebox (they recently converted to CD format).

DUX'S
CAJUN

While sports bars are as common a sight these days as shaved-headed black men, the *Cajun* sports bar remains a far rarer bird. In the case of Dux's, the food is the distinguishing characteristic that sets it apart from umpteen other places where a world without ESPN is a world gone horribly wrong. It also differs from its heart-of-Buckhead neighbors in that it makes little attempt at a high profile—it's up a little hill with an unmarked narrow driveway snaking around to a rear parking lot.

AND THE BREAKFAST, SIMPLE AS IT WAS, I COULD NOT HAVE HAD AT ANY RESTAURANT IN ATLANTA AT ANY PRICE. THERE WAS FRIED CHICKEN, AS IT IS FRIED ONLY IN THE SOUTH, HOMINY BOILED TO THE CONSISTENCY WHERE IT COULD BE EATEN WITH A FORK, AND BISCUITS SO LIGHT AND FLAKY THAT A FELLOW WITH ANY APPETITE AT ALL WOULD HAVE NO DIFFICULTY IN DISPOSING OF EIGHT OR TEN.

James Weldon Johnson
The Autobiography of
an Ex-Coloured Man
(1912)

248 PHARR ROAD
BUCKHEAD
404-814-0558
11:30A-2:30P,
6P-11P TUE-THU
11:30A-2:30P,
6P-12P FRI
12P-12A SAT
12P-11P SUN
V/MC/AMEX

Lunch kicks off around 11:30 but they usually move a little slow before noon. Specials, which change daily, are about $7, but you'll be most likely to feel as if someone colored you with the Happy Crayon when ordering the spicy breaded catfish or shrimp poor boy. Unless you're positively ravenous, a half boy ($6) is plenty, as it's served with a choice of red beans and rice, gumbo, or jambalaya (beans are the way to go here).

The dinner meal adds some impressive entrees such as blackened ribeye steak ($16) and deep-fried softshell crabs that could set Justin Wilson's suspenders to snapping something ferocious. After putting an edge on your palate with a dark Abita Turbodog beer (served on tap), you can keep a lean tab by ordering a poor boy or the blackened chicken salad, a deal at six bills.

For an appetizer, try the hot 'n cheddary crawfish dip (served with tortilla chips) or the marinated alligator bites, tinged with cayenne and sauteed in butter. Further down the menu, two dessert offerings ($3.95) stand apart from the crowd, namely the bread pudding with rum sauce (a bayou favorite) and the deep-dish Bourbon Street pecan pie—made with decent whiskey and topped with a scoop of praline ice cream. Sweet ain't the word.

(CAJUN) IS A DISTINCT CUISINE THAT CAN BE MIGHTY TASTY, EVEN IF DONE TO DEATH BY LOCAL PREMIX ENTREPRENEURS AND BY GIMMICK-HAPPY YANKEE CHEFS WHO WOULD BLACKEN A DOORSTOP IF THEY THOUGHT SOMEBODY WOULD BUY IT AND EAT IT.

Chris Maynard and Bill Scheller
Manifold Destiny
(1989)

EAST VILLAGE GRILLE

COMFORT FOOD

If you find yourself in Buckhead during the wee hours, needful of sustenance and unopposed to the prospect of crossing paths with more than a few *Friends* wannabes, point yourself toward this towering structure. Although it's one of the more overtly yuppie hangouts you'll encounter during most of the day and into the evening, the Grille's straight Southern menu is as remarkable for its quality as for its lack of pretense.

Now going on a decade old, East Village is the budget-level offering of highly successful restaurateur George Rohrig, otherwise known for his spendier establishments, Azio's and Otto's among them. Savvy chap that he is, Rohrig brought in head cook Antoinette Lloyd—formerly of the Peachtree Cafe, if that means anything to you—to oversee the kitchen at what is, in most other respects, an upscale sports bar. It has since become something of a magnet for Atlanta's under-30 set, who gather to rub Brooks Brothers-clad shoulders and introduce their tastebuds to good scotch.

Lunches and dinners ($7-$10) are strictly stick-to-the-ribs fare, with daily specials that include homemade chicken pot pies, dense meatloaf and skillet-fried chicken, all of which rank with the best in the city. Fleshing out the menu are an assortment of huge hamburgers and sandwiches (the club being a particular standout), each served with a couple of fresh vegetables, fries or salad. A plentiful late-night breakfast is quite popular and gets

248 Buckhead Ave.
Buckhead
404-233-3345
11a-12-a Sun-Thu
11a-4a Fri-Sat
V/MC/AMEX

He who dines latest is the greatest man; and he who dines earliest is accounted the least.

Herman Melville
White Jacket (1850)

going as need demands—usually about 9:30 or 10 p.m. Plunk down your $2.99 and say howdy to a platter of scrambled eggs, hashbrowns, bacon and a honking big buttermilk biscuit. No substitutions. It's a sweet deal if you're already winding up your evening in Buckhead, but not worth a special trip as you're liable blow a fair wad on parking at that hour.

EAT'S
PASTA & JERK CHICKEN

600 PONCE DE LEON AVE.
404-888-9149
11A-10P DAILY
NO PLASTIC

As the stripped down name intimates, this place is an unvarnished alternative to Atlanta's bevy of eateries whose stabs at creating atmosphere are often too cute by half. Had Thoreau decided to go into the food service biz this is likely the sort of place he would have come up with, an expertly minimalist joint with bare wooden floors and chairs and little else in the way of adornment. The menu is likewise simple, albeit in a way more curious than the decor, with the focus on pasta, jerk chicken and Southern style vegetables. Unorthodox, yes, but it works.

Pastawise, choices range across the semolina spectrum—from linguine to cheese-filled spinach tortellini. They toss your noodles into boiling water while you choose a sauce: marinara (with or without ground turkey), alfredo, pesto or olive oil and garlic. Not a dud in the lot, and the price tag is a cool $4 (including garlic bread). If it's jerk chicken you're after, mosey on to the back for a half bird with two veggies—there's usually a selection of eight or so, highlighted by simmered collard greens and corn on the cob—and crumbly yellow cornbread for $5, day or night.

After filling your plate (despite appearances, it's not an all-you-can-eat type deal), help yourself to a beverage—soda, tea, wine or beer. If you're partial to the latter, they offer a goodly assortment of imports at reasonable prices; a Bass Ale, for example, will run you $2.15. Grab a homemade brownie if they've got 'em: be nice and they might just slide you a chewy corner piece and maybe even let you burp the Tupperware container.

EINSTEIN'S

SANDWICHES

If all it had going for it was the city's best outdoor eating area—50 or so tables, with bright red, blue and yellow chairs—this place would still be worth a visit. Factor in cheap food in prodigious portions, though, and even the village idiot can recognize Einstein's considerable appeal. Devotees of the place recommend it with an almost religious fervor, and their numbers are such that the owners eventually expanded into the two adjacent addresses. And lately, they've even solved the one problem that plagued them for years: parking.

Once you find a spot—most likely across the street—you can, if snacking is in the game plan, tee off with an order of sweet Coconut Shrimp (deep-fried and served with orange-flavored honey mustard) or skewered Sesame Chicken with a ginger yogurt sauce (both are about $7). Pasta is done with flair, particularly the Cajun chicken linguine (a cayenne-spiked cream sauce tossed with breast meat, fresh tomatoes and green onions). If you

1077 Juniper St.
Midtown
404-876-7925
11a-12a Sun-Thu
11a-1a Fri-Sat
V/MC/AMEX

fancy The Other White Meat, go with the chutney-topped grilled pork chop; for fish lovers, the tomatoey trout is fine stuff, with a heavy blast of basil. On the meatless side, they have an upscale stir fry (with porto bello mushrooms and snap peas, over wild rice).

The menu highlights, though, are without a doubt the sandwiches. Huge, creatively preparedwonders they are, served with a mound of shoestring sweet potato fries and begging for your attention. The house specialty is the Einstein Grille, smoked turkey, bacon and tomato on egg-battered sourdough with a sexy raspberry sauce on the side. While relatively pricey at $7.50, it's indisputably a mother of a sandwich. Their flamboyant interpretation of the Reuben (comprised of a grilled chicken breast on thick rye, smothered with Swiss cheese, cole slaw and thousand island dressing) is inspired if not exactly tidy.

El Charro
MEXICAN

2581 PIEDMONT ROAD
NE ATLANTA
404-264-0613
9:30A-10P DAILY
V/MC

Wedged betwixt a check-cashing enterprise and a balloon delivery store—hey, man, it's Atlanta—El Charro is a dependable outlet for quality Mexican eats. And while it's exterior may be so inocuous as to border on snooze-inducing, the dozen-booth interior exhibits far more personality. The overall effect can at times be downright cheery, what with the vibrantly colored knickknacks and the constant thrum of the all-Latino jukebox.

Lunch combinations are as reasonable as they come at around $4, comprised of standard fare such as tacos, enchiladas and chile rellenos—all done with a very high level of competence. That said, it's the dinners which really shine, from the bargain-priced choriqueso (a baked cheese-and-chorizo-sausage hybrid, served in a shallow ceramic bowl) to the gringas (flour tortillas blanketing a baked blend of spicy ground beef and white cheese) to chicken ladled with a sublime mole sauce (made from ground pumpkin seeds and unsweetened chocolate). The broiled shrimp with salsa can also be quite striking, as can the combination fajitas (chicken, shrimp and steak), which represent the north end of the price range at $10.

Over on the liquid side, you'll find a roster of Mexican and American beers along with a rather inspired margarita, made with white wine. It's their own recipe, and it gives the old favorite a sort of Bartles & Jaymes-meets-Jimmy Buffett type of feel—not for all tastes, certainly, but surprisingly good. Desserts consist of the standards, both done quite nicely—sopapillas cowering beneath a hail of powdered sugar, and creamy flan sporting a light jacket of caramel sauce.

El Salvador
SALVADORAN

Aside from this nifty little Salvadoran eatery, Northeast Plaza is most notable for its $1.50 cinema. The films lean far further in the direction of 90 minutes of Steven Seagal (no Jackie Chan, even) kicking ass and taking names than Jane Austen adaptations, so proceed as you see fit. At any rate, there's little doubt that if you have an interest in good eats, you should forego the oily popcorn and check out El Salvador before, after, or—if you have a large coat—during your movie.

THE MISER'S FEAST IS OFTEN THE MOST SPLENDID.

Samuel Richardson
Sir Charles Grandison
(1749)

3375 BUFORD HIGHWAY
NE ATLANTA
404-325-0482
11:30A-11:30P DAILY
V/MC

To keep your mind off Junior Mints for a good long while, get into a sizeable spit-roasted chicken (tender meat stripped from the bone and topped with fresh cilantro) or the ribeye sandwich, served on a grilled roll.

The vegetarian combination plate is a terrific option, equipped with a potato burrito (again, heavy on the cilantro) filled with big chunks o' spud along with sauteed onions and green peppers. Fluffy rice and refried beans give the platters a nice balanced look that would bring a smile to the face of any home ec teacher. For under four bucks you can also get some nicely done straight Mexican standards: two enchiladas, rice, and beans, or a platter of huevos rancheros (two eggs smothered in a homemade salsa that will set your ears to ringing).

Dinnertime-only standouts include the $7 pollo campesino (a boneless breast topped with ham, a fried egg, and a good shot of salsa), a gigantic chimichanga, and the excellent chuzos (grilled beef kebobs with green peppers, onions, tomatoes and mushrooms). In keeping with the neighbors, the interior is no great shakes, defined primarily by a few doodads from the homeland and a fleet of booths that look to have come straight from a bankruptcy auction. The proprietors, by contrast, are a class act, outgoing without being smothering.

I'M NOT VORACIOUS; ONLY PECKISH.

Miguel de Cervantes
Don Quixote (1605-15)

EVANS FINE FOODS
COMFORT FOOD

Guided by the steady hand of their father Spyros—he ran the Atlanta Steakhouse for nearly 30 years—brothers Mike and Pete Kontoes have done well for themselves since buying out the Evans family in 1982. Though their new building lacks the worn character of the original, Evans' still serves up the soul-stirring comfort food that has kept many a distraught Emory freshman from bagging his classes mid-quarter and signing on as a carnival worker.

While nestling into a springy naugahyde booth, cast a sharp eye in the direction of the chalkboard menu. There you'll find a slew of lunch and dinner specials (about $5); the worst of the bunch can still seem like a visit to Dr. Feelgood, but take particular note of the meatloaf, beef stew, country-fried steak, fried flounder, and the roast pork and cornbread dressing.

All entrees come with rolls and a pair of vegetables, among which the yams, mashed potatoes and green beans are particular hotshots, though everything is remarkably consistent. Consequently, the vegetable plates, which also come with rolls or cornbread, are a gold mine at under four bucks. Other fare includes competent standards like a chef's salad (topped with strips of ham and turkey, shredded cheddar and hardboiled eggs) and homemade tuna salad (a couple of big scoops on a bed of lettuce).

Among the top draws at Evans' are the pies and cobblers, created on site and not a whit shy of

2125 NORTH
DECATUR ROAD
EMORY AREA
404-634-6294
5:30A-9P MON-SAT
NO PLASTIC

NEARLY EVERYONE WANTS AT LEAST ONE OUTSTANDING MEAL A DAY.

Duncan Hines
Adventures in Good
Eating (1936)

fantastic. Provided your waitress can hear your inquiry over the meal-hour tumult, she'll point you in the direction of that day's best dessert bet—they usually have both blackberry and peach cobbler (topped with a buttery crust) as well as chocolate, apple and coconut cream pies (about a buck and a half per slice, with whole pies a mere $7).

Feeders For BBQ

BARBECUE

1999 CHESHIRE
BRIDGE ROAD
NE ATLANTA
404-872-8488
11:30A-9P MON-SAT
V/MC

Perennial cookoff entrants Marty Boyd and Rick Young are hammering away at any preconceived notions Atlantans may harbor regarding what a barbecue restaurant should be. Besides putting the fire to a solid roster of ribs, pulled pork, beef brisket and smoked chicken, they take a few remarkably refreshing steps outside the usual conventions of the industry.

Takeout is popular, but you'll also find a steady stream of lunchtime regulars piling into the modest dining room (there's also a side deck). These folks find more than ample motivation in the form of sandwiches loaded with tender pork or smoked chicken salad (chicken, onions and celery tossed with mayo), as well as thick fries and some raging Buffalo wings (drumettes, actually). For dinner ($6-$8), draw a bead on virtually any pork or beef (the ribs and brisket are both prime) offering, or the rib and chicken combo—half a spice-rubbed bird, a pile of ribs, and two side dishes. The tangy cole slaw, Brunswick stew and yam-pecan casserole rate as the best of a generally commendable lot.

As intriguing as anything you'll encounter in the wide world of barbecue is Feeders' smoked duck. If most of their other meat offerings show some level of restraint, here they let their culinary hair down til it's piling around their ankles, basting these quackers with a medley of offbeat sauces incorporating everything from mangoes and bourbon to a strawberry daiquiri.

In this same innovative vein is the Hall of Flame, offered every other Tuesday and Wednesday night (two seatings—7 and 8:30 p.m.—by reservation only). This little soiree highlights fire-loving cuisines, and features Thai, Ethiopian and Caribbean dishes whipped up with true flair. In the manner of many an Asian or African cook, Boyd has as much pride in the spice rubs, sauces and other condiments of his own devising—beware the cripplingly hot habanero salsa—as he does in his main courses. And if you're game for a little pre-dinner mandibular challenge, get busy on a wrinkly strap of his homemade beef jerky.

POULTRY IS FOR THE COOK WHAT CANVAS IS FOR THE PAINTER.

Anthelme Brillat-Savarin
The Physiology of Taste
(1825)

FELLINI'S
PIZZA

923 Ponce de Leon Ave.
Poncey-Highlands
404-873-3088

422 Seminole Ave.
Little Five Points
404-525-2530

2809 Peachtree Road
Buckhead
404-266-0082

4429 Roswell Road
Buckhead
404-303-8248

1991 Howell Mill Road
NW Atlanta
404-352-0799

1634 McLendon Ave.
Candler Park
404-687-9190

11:30a-2a Daily
(McLendon Ave: 11a-12a)
No Plastic

Fellini's is perhaps the city's prime spot for people with straight jobs and conventional haircuts to nosh cheek by jowl with Atlanta's burgeoning legion of slackers. At the vortex of this curious little universe is some A-kicking, New York-style pizza that ranks with the finest thin crust pies you're likely to find anywhere near this far south. Although the original location next to Garden Hills Cinema has been converted into a LaFonda Cantina—another venture by Fellini's owners Mike Nelson and Clay Harper—the frenzied, come-as-everyone-else-ain't spirit that was birthed back in the mid-eighties is alive and well, and now living at groovy locations all around town.

Noncircular offerings like the sizeable calzones ($5) and the salads are respectable, make no mistake, but the pizzas stand alone in terms of desirability. For around $14 bucks—about what you net for a plasma donation—they'll whip up a large pie with a couple of toppings (meatballs and green peppers make an especially comely pair). If that's too much of a commitment, you can get it by the slice, for about $1.50 per. After you order, they'll hand you a lucite-encased postcard (featuring everyone from Zippy the Pinhead to Muddy Waters) and bid you find a table. To slake your thirst, have 'em draw a pitcher of Rolling Rock (draft beers vary by location) or grab one of those big oil cans of Foster's Lager.

There's remarkably little variation in quality amongst the Fellinis, but the people-watching is usually best at the Little Five Points location, where a pair of Doc Martens are practically as viable a currency as anything bearing the image of a dead president. The stereo blares as loudly as ever, but unfortunately their supergroovy patio seating is no more (there's still a small area of covered outdoor dining), thanks reportedly to a city official who thought it projected a bad image. Blame it on The Man.

FIESTA FOODS
CARIBBEAN

For the past eight years, this little grocery has been serving up to-go lunches that are touchstones of artistic simplicity. Since their recent move to a nicer space around the corner, they've also begun offering an arresting sitdown menu; the splendid takeout sandwiches remain the main attraction, however, and most days their assembly keeps owner Amar Bayzid as busy as any guy this side of Art Schlicter's bookie.

For $3.50 a pop, you have your choice of three sandwiches—Cuban, cheese (containing a generous wad of mozzarella), or rotisserie-cooked chicken—on a crunchy loaf that's grilled into a state of immoderate flatness. The Cuban sandwich is a textbook rendition, featuring a foundation of succulent roast pork festooned with mild green chiles, a munificent sprinkling of cilantro and lettuce, and a heavy dose of mojo sauce (an herbed oil and vinegar dressing). If you want a little more variety for about the same price, try a half sandwich combo, including salsa-basted rice, beans and iced tea.

2581 PIEDMONT ROAD
NE ATLANTA
404-237-7308
9A-8P DAILY
NO PLASTIC

Sandwiches aside, Fiesta is also well worth knowing about if you fancy yourself handy in the kitchen. While they're wrapping up your order, stroll the wide aisles and check out the selection, ranging from a full complement of Goya brand products—canned pigeon peas, tamales, plantain chips—to frozen banana leaves and champagne-flavored sodas. There's also much in the way of bulk foods to interest the Spanish cook—not leastly, of course, an array of chile peppers, which they stock by the barrelful.

On your way out, pick up a green "lucky lotto" candle (can't hurt, right?) and check to see if they have any freshly baked treats—the sugar-crusted apple and cherry tarts ($1.50) make an especially nice accompaniment to a sandwich.

FLYING BISCUIT CAFE

BREAKFAST & SANDWICHES

1655 McLENDON AVE.
CANDLER PARK
404-687-8888
8:30A-10:30P TUE-SUN
(BAKERY OPENS AT 7:30A)
V/MC/AMEX

Two years ago, from the ashes of Sylvia's Atomic Cafe arose the Flying Biscuit, an unpretentious and inexpensive bistro. What with the fine eats and the lively decor (handpainted sunflowers cover the walls), the Biscuit quickly gained a following; thanks primarily to great word-of-mouth, it has since grown into an 80-table operation with a rear deck and an in-house bakery turning out all manner of pastries and breads.

There are, as one might surmise, biscuits at the center of the action. Qualitywise, they rank high enough to have you laughing yourself silly at all future mentions of the name "Hungry Jack." All breakfasts come with a puck-sized biscuit and rosemary-dusted, oven-roasted potatoes. The Flying

Biscuit Breakfast, featuring a pair of brown eggs (not that you can tell without the shell, of course), and turkey sausages humming with sage, is but one of a pack of comely morning meal options. Also great are the organic oatmeal pancakes, topped

with warm peach compote, and the Meggxican Wrap, a figurative and literal mouthful comprised of stylishly prepared huevos rancheros swaddled in a flour tortilla.

Under the all-inclusive Sandwich heading, you'll find two surefire selections, namely the spicy black bean quesadilla and the Angel Burger, a veggie and grain patty with a generous layer of roasted red pepper mustard. The vegetarian soups have both delighted and disappointed, so gamble as you see fit. There's no rolling the bones when it comes to the house salad, though; it's always steady and comes, like damn near everything but dessert, with a biscuit.

Occupying the north end of the scale in terms of price and sheer substance is the $8 turkey meatloaf and Pudge (a bed of mashed red potatoes infused with sundried tomatoes, basil, and olive oil). The Love Cakes (black bean patties) and the Virtuous Vegan Pie (a dairy-free quiche) are liable to be of interest only to non-carnivores. Beveragewise, you'll find iced herbal teas, sodas and flavored waters, beer and wine. If you're of a particularly steely mind, order the Bohemian Breakfast, a demitasse of espresso and two cigarettes—served for the road only, since the Biscuit bans butts.

THERE IS NOTHING SO BEAUTIFUL THAT IT WILL MAKE PEOPLE FORGET THEIR EGGS AND BACON FOR BREAKFAST.

Charlie Chaplin quoted in Clare Sheridan's *My American Diary* (1922)

FRENCH QUARTER GROCERY
CAJUN & CREOLE

923 PEACHTREE ST.
MIDTOWN
404-875-2489

2144 JOHNSON
FERRY ROAD
BROOKHAVEN
770-458-2148

11A-10P MON-THU
11A-11P FRI-SAT
V/MC/AMEX

Sad fact though it is, you won't find many places outside of Louisiana serving authentic Cajun food as delectable as that at the French Quarter. Even with the addition of a covered curbside patio, this family-run Midtown joint is a little deficient as far as seating goes, but the dining experience is such that a 20-minute wait is to be blithely endured. To pass the time, check out the small grocery area stocked with Cajun Power (a hot garlic sauce) and Zapp's crawfish-flavored potato chips.

Lunch is great, but evening provides the prime opportunity for a Crescent City bender. Pre-entree courses include shrimp creole, a seafood etoufee, and expertly fried shrimp or oysters with a side of remoulade sauce (a mayo-based potion jazzed with cayenne). Each day they also prepare either a soup (along the lines of alligator stew or oyster bisque) or a gumbo (duck or chicken) which is rarely short of outstanding. No less compelling are the meal-sized salads, including the spectacular boiled shrimp version (sporting a provocative wig of Mandarin oranges and toasted pecans, drizzled with remoulade), and the fried oysters sprawled on a mattress of fresh spinach with a parmesan and peppercorn dressing.

The oversized poor boy sandwiches—sided with a dish of killer red beans and rice—may be enough to have you putting the house up for sale and scanning the New Orleans want ads. Fillings abound, including fried shrimp, oysters, or catfish (yes, yes, and y-y-yes), as well as andouille sausage or smoked turkey. That other Big Easy trademark sandwich, the muffuletta—baked ham, salami, cheeses and antipasti stuffed into a fat boule loaf—also gets the royal treatment.

If you make it that far, full meals are certifiably gigantic and an intoxicating bargain at under $10. Fried softshell crabs stuffed with crawfish in a garlic cream sauce are a scintillating highlight; several other seafood and steak platters are also worthwhile, if hopelessly mundane by comparison. Cap your meal with a serving of warm bread pudding (crammed with raisins, pecans and pineapple and with bourbon sauce), or a slice of pecan praline cheesecake (don't expect this one to sit too light).

NEW ORLEANS IN SPRING-TIME, JUST WHEN THE ORCHARDS WERE FLUSHING OVER WITH PEACH-BLOS-SOMS, AND THE SWEET HERBS CAME TO FLA-VOR THE JULIPS—SEEMED TO ME THE CITY OF THE WORLD WHERE YOU CAN EAT AND DRINK THE MOST AND SUFFER THE LEAST.

William Makepeace Thackeray (1862)

FRIJOLERO'S

TEX-MEX

Thanks to their emphasis on large portions at next-to-nothing prices, this gringo-run Texican joint has become a darling of the young and the thin of wallet. While the sign reminding patrons to place their orders under the "Order Here" sign may have you doubting the clientele's cognitive abilities, there's no arguing that they've zeroed in on a winner.

The upholstery is fake snakeskin, the music straight out of Athens (Georgia, that is), and, in a manner faintly reminiscent of The Varsity, the person taking your order is quite apt to have indifference rising off their body like steam. Likely as not they'll greet you with a half-hearted "Hey. Whaddaya want?", a question which can be surprisingly hard to answer given the complex combinations of Mexican-inspired fare.

1031 PEACHTREE ST.
MIDTOWN
404-892-8226
11A-12A MON-THU
11A-1A FRI
12P-1A SAT
12P-12A SUN
NO PLASTIC

If you're powerful hungry, the burritos are the ticket. The $3.50 meatless version consists of a steamed flour tortilla chocked with pinto beans, rice, jack cheese, salsa and green chilies—to say it is as big as your forearm would be only the slightest of exaggerations. For an extra buck or so they'll fatten it up even further, with either beef or barbecued chicken. While exponentially smaller, the tacos are no less enticing and come served in the simple Mexican style: open-faced on a grilled corn tortilla, with the same ingredients you'll find in the burritos.

Beyond the basics, there's a tempting assortment of other options, including barbecued chicken fajitas, a sizeable chalupa with a fiery, chunky guacamole, a tasty grilled chicken salad, and a vegetarian green chili stew full of corn, zucchini, and red and yellow sweet peppers that's served over rice and flat-out terrific.

FUZZY'S PLACE
ECLECTIC AMERICAN

Building upon its decade-long success as both a friendly watering hole and a proving ground for the city's indigenous musical talent, Fuzzy's has of late transformed its once unspectacular smattering of bar food. Not that you would guess it by outward appearances—it still has "dive" written all over it, with darkly tinted windows and more than its share of good-natured barflies.

But back in the kitchen, change has been a'brewing. If you live in these parts and do any serious grilling on the homefront, you're likely familiar with Joe Dale's Smokehouse Marinade, an

2015 NORTH DRUID HILLS ROAD
NE ATLANTA
404-321-6166
11A-4A MON-SAT
12:30P-4A SUN
V/MC/AMEX

all-purpose cooking sauce of the highest caliber. The man behind that thin, dark elixir was a popular Atlanta restaurateur for 40 years, after which he spent nearly a decade in retirement; alas, the call of the commercial kitchen eventually proved irresistible, and since 1994 Dale has worked his culinary magic at Fuzzy's stove. Hence the rebirth of the menu.

The options changes daily as new ideas are tried and tweaked. For lunch and dinner, they offer up about seven entrees and a soup du jour—of course, phrases like "du jour" seem a little preposterous in a place where the central item of decor is a mural of a '57 Chevy. At any rate, the creamy chicken and pasta soup is a standout, and among the headliners you want to be watching for the grilled salmon, smoked oysters or grilled Italian sausage and peppers over penne pasta with a basil-heavy tomato sauce. Not too shabby for a place with one of those tabletop shuffleboard machines.

WO WAS HIS COOK, IF HIS SAUCE WAS NOT POYNAUNT AND SHARP.

Geoffrey Chaucer
Canterbury Tales (c. 1395)

GARAM
KOREAN

Along a two-mile stretch of Buford Highway just beyond I-285, you'll find perhaps a dozen Korean restaurants turning out "Seoul" food of drastically varying degrees of quality. For the uninitiated, discerning the best of the bunch can be edifying, to say the least. If you'd like to skip the rather involved research, though, let there be no doubt that Garam is as good as it gets.

As is often the case with Korean eateries, the building's exterior is somewhat dumpy—flaking paint and a parking lot in need of some serious

5881 BUFORD HWY.
DORAVILLE
770-454-9198
10:30A-12A DAILY
V/MC/AMEX

gardening—but it's comfortable and tidy once you're through the door. All the karaoke equipment—seemingly as critical to a Korean evening out as, say, pants—is discreetly shoved aside for the lunch crowds. But come sundown, private parties are invited to crank it up, and many are the nights when the walls reverberate with heavily accented refrains of "Burning Love."

The three cavernous dining rooms contain oversized booths, yet leggy diners may find them cruelly reminiscent of riding in a Le Car. The deceptively cramped quarters are to the built-in tabletop grills, central to a popular bit of feasting called yakiniku. Perhaps a little time-prohibitive for lunch, the sensual orgy of slow-grilling marinated meats (gingery beef, peppery pork, and shrimp) and vegetables makes for a thoroughly satisfying dinner.

EATING IS HEAVEN.

Korean proverb

Like most East Asians, Koreans are a soup-crazed lot. Garam's are exceptional, served in bowls so alarmingly deep you'll be tempted to tote along your hip waders. Of particular note are the beefy sul rung tang and the kal guk soo (chicken with broad rice noodles). Also excellent are the $5 Lunch Box specials (similar to Japanese bentos). Salmon, soy-marinated ribeye slices, and beef short ribs are all done nicely; kim chee items along for the ride include chilled noodles, sticky rice, gingery shreds of meat and cabbage, sweet and sour dried sardines, and cold greens with sesame oil. Don't expect to be offered a fork—it's chopsticks all the way.

GORIN'S
ICE CREAM

It's no surprise that in a city where summers are notoriously punishing, an enterprise cranking out dozens of premium ice creams would thrive. It is something of a wonder, however, that there aren't more establishments vying for a scoop of the action. Gorin's stands as the undisputed king of fine frozen treats hereabouts; fortunately, they wears the crown with style, maintaining a high level of consistency even while continuing to spread like kudzu across the Atlanta area (they also have outposts in Alabama and North Carolina).

Hewing to the traditional ice cream parlor theme, the decor is kind of cutesy in a uniform, nondescript sort of way. For those looking for an actual meal, they offer a few salads and a wide selection of tasty (but smallish) sandwiches. Best of the lot is the chunky Almond Chicken Melt on grilled egg bread.

Needless to report, though, frozen confections are the main attraction. Each day, they inscribe a large chalkboard with the day's 15 or so hand-stirred ice creams, sherbets and frozen yogurts. Longtime favorites like Oreo, amaretto almond and mint chocolate chip are supplemented by more sporadically produced flavors like banana pudding (with whole vanilla wafers) and raspberries and cream.

If you like to play the fat-free game, their selection of yogurts—caramel pecan, chocolate almond and strawberry peach, to name a few—bearing that label are also worth a try. Definitely not as flavorful

620 PEACHTREE ST.
MIDTOWN
404-874-0550
9:30A-5P MON-FRI
10A-6P SAT-SUN

(MORE THAN 20 OTHER LOCATIONS INCLUDING CNN CENTER, AREA MALLS AND UNDERGROUND ATLANTA)
HOURS VARY

I DOUBT THE WORLD HOLDS FOR ANYONE A MORE SOUL-STIRRING SURPRISE THAN THE FIRST ADVENTURE WITH ICE CREAM

Heywood Broun
(1888-1939)

as the genuine article, and a smidgeon on the icy side, but that's the way the world works. Beyond the usual cones, the creamy stuff is available in numerous other guises, from a mortar-thick milkshake ($2.50) to the two-scoop banana split.

GRANDMA'S BISCUITS
MEAT-&-THREE

5880 BUFORD HIGHWAY
DORAVILLE
770-458-4553
6A-9P MON-FRI
6A-8P SAT
8A-3P SUN
NO PLASTIC

IN HEAVEN I HOPE TO BAKE MY OWN BREAD AND CLEAN MY OWN LINEN.

Henry David Thoreau
Journal (1841)

Although Korean restaurants dominate this zip code, Grandma's routinely draws a bigger lunch crowd than any of them. Everyone from local boy mechanics to big-haired secretaries to the ocassional kim-chee-weary immigrant descends on this log cabin come noontime, looking for serious Southern eats served up family reunion-style (read: on styrofoam plates).

Up on the big board, you'll be offered a choice between a Small Lunch ($5), a Big Lunch ($6), or a vegetable plate for $4. Think you can remember that? As far as entrees go, several daily specials are offered along with the perennial favorite, fried chicken. Jump at the chance to get the beef tips over rice or the piquant barbecued beef ribs. The vegetables are fresh and consistently good, from the lightly breaded fried okra to the macaroni and cheese (very much a vegetable in the Southern scheme) and the tender green beans. The sweet potato souffle, whipped smooth and full of pecans, also ranks right up there and could serve just as well as a dessert—banish the thought, however, as you'd have to be a bit touched in the head to bypass their blackberry or peach cobbler.

As the name alludes, biscuits get big play here. You'll be happy to learn that they're well worth trying, with a crumbly outer crust. Unless you specify otherwise, they come pre-split and buttered. On subsequent visits, however, give the slightly sweet cornbread a shake, as it's every bit as fine. If the weather's cooperative, skip the crowded dining room and take your grub out to one of the picnic tables on the mammoth front porch.

GRANT CENTRAL PIZZA & PASTA

PIZZA

The Grant Park community was widely considered a real estate gamble several years back, but those who bought into its potential as the next restoration hotbed have since realized a huge upside. As the beautiful old homes have been rehabbed and the neighborhood has grown in popularity, new businesses have begun sprouting left and right. Strategically located on the park's north edge, Grant's got in early, and has since cultivated a reputation for terrific thin-crust pizzas in the Fellini's mold, albeit amid slightly more subdued environs.

Situated in an old brick storefront that has been given the requisite facelift, Grant's is cozy without being cramped. Seat yourself at one of the 10 or so tables (with mismatched floral tablecloths) or in one of the big semicircular booths. You'll find the menu written on a huge blackboard, and once you've ordered scope out the groovy old Seebury High Fidelity jukebox, endowed with a commendably eclectic selection of 45s (Tom Jones

451 CHEROKEE AVE.
GRANT PARK
404-523-8900
11:30A-10P MON-FRI
5P-10P SAT

1279 GLENWOOD AVE.
EAST ATLANTA
404-627-0007
11A-12A DAILY

V/MC

to Louis Armstrong). For entertainment of a more passive variety, check out their ever-growing collection of Pez dispensers.

The slightly chewy, New York-style pizzas ($9 large, $1.35 a slice) are served on a metal pan covered with a sheet of wax paper. They come with your choice of additions for $1.25 each; beyond the usual choices, you'll find thick-sliced meatballs, sun-dried tomatoes, breaded eggplant, and potato chunks swabbed with an oregano/basil/red pepper mixture. The $4 calzones (crammed with cheese and your favorite meat—the Italian sausage is prime) and the pasta dishes (fettucine or linguine with cream, marinara or pesto sauces) are winners one and all. Portions are uniformly generous, so grab a basket of garlic bread only if you're ravenous.

GREENWOOD'S ON GREEN STREET

COMFORT FOOD

1087 GREEN ST.
ROSWELL
404-523-8030
5P-9P MON-THU
5P-10P FRI-SAT
NO PLASTIC

It's worth every mile and wrong turn you'll make on the way to this little one-story house, where they serve up Southern food of impeccable pedigree. What's more, the portions are doubtless the heftiest you'll see where there's not a grandmama involved, and this way you run no risk of having to endure *Lawrence Welk* reruns.

Though the service is generally snappy, getting a table can involve a wait. Meanwhile, the pie-cooling rack is right in front of you. It's OK to stare. The four dining rooms have well-traveled hardwood floors and cement-chinked walls meant to resemble the interior of a log cabin. While scarfing a moist, white corn muffin, you can either scan the menu or simply watch the deft waitresses hauling out comfort food by the luscious trayful. First-timers are recognizable by their blinking double-takes—that's no booster seat, friend, it's a slab of meatloaf.

Among the fine entrees (most in the $8 range) are two huge, lightly breaded boneless pork chops sauteed in butter—that's right, butter—or the half-chicken, shiny with a glaze of barely sweet plum sauce. The fried chicken is also quite bodacious, but they tell you right up front that it'll take a good half-hour to cook. Of course, you could use that time to get to know one (or more) of their estimable microbrews, including Dubuque Big Muddy, an unfiltered red ale.

For your two side orders, choose from the 10 or so regular options. The mashed potatoes and the chunky, cinnamon-dusted applesauce are two to think about; the lone disappointment is the lemon juice-drenched collards, which miss the mark entirely. To put a cap on things, the pies are a must. Slices are a mite steep at $4, but, if you call ahead, they will send you home with a whole one for a ten-spot. The apple version is topped with a thin veneer of pastry, and the chocolate pie is nothing short of a work of art, covered with fresh whipped cream and semi-sweet shavings. Bring your camera.

VEGETABLES ARE INTERESTING BUT LACK A SENSE OF PURPOSE WHEN UNACCOMPANIED BY A GOOD CUT OF MEAT.

Fran Lebowitz
Metropolitan Life
(1978)

HAPPY HERMAN'S
SANDWICHES

2299 CHESHIRE
BRIDGE ROAD
NE ATLANTA
404-321-3012

7291 NORTH POINT PKWY.
ALPHARETTA
770-993-4770

204 JOHNSON FERRY RD.
SANDY SPRINGS
770-256-3354

9A-9P MON-THU
9A-10P FRI-SAT
10A-6P SUN
V/MC

To look at the neighborhood surrounding the original Herman's in Northeast Atlanta, you'd think that folks around here were more interested in plunking down their hard-earned moolah for a couch dance than a gourmet sandwich. Apparently it's not viewed as an either-or proposition, though, as business is hopping at this fancy food shop, shining like a waystation of good living amid the garish mosaic of neon and blinking signs.

Everything on the menu is available for takeout, but there's also a small indoor dining area and an outside deck with several large tables. The Cuban sandwiches are pre-made and merely adequate, but most any of the other 20-plus alternatives are excellent, almost comically overstuffed, and priced right (under $5). The four-inch-high Colossal Club (a boule loaf heaped with turkey, ham, bacon and your choice of cheese) is a looker, as is the classy tuna salad (white albacore in a light mayo dressing with a hint of dill). They also fashion obscenely plump sandwiches from baked ham, turkey breast, corned beef and flank steak, all of which are sliced to order at their fancy carving station.

For roughage you can choose from several large salads, including a single-serving caesar they'll whip up before your eyes. These are complemented nicely by a square of focaccia. The ready-made entrees are also of a high grade, led by the splendid rosemary roasted chicken. Nifty meal accessories to be found among the exotic pates and Toblerone chocolates include ginger beer and bags of sweet-potato chips. Or, if the latter don't exactly put a crease in your britches, try the extra-crunchy Taste of the Orient potato chips (the hot mustard flavor is especially terrific). And at least while the fad lasts, you can wind up your visit with a fine cigar—they've added a humidor packed with more than 50 kinds.

HAROLD'S BARBECUE
BARBECUE

Just up the road from the federal penitentiary, Don Hembree continues to stoke the fire that his daddy, Harold, sparked nearly 50 years ago. Over the decades, father and son have earned a reputation for slow-cooked pork of surpassing quality, served in a setting characterized by framed religious tracts and a clientele of serious eaters, more than few of whom bear a marked resemblance to that jiggly guy who played the mayor on *Carter Country.*

Depending on when you drop in, you may have to hang out for a seat; not to worry, though, as there's a cavernous back dining room in addition to the dozen tables up front, so any line you encounter will move quickly. The menu is replete with such drive-in mainstays as grilled hot dogs

I LIKE THE PHILOSO-PHY OF THE SANDWICH, AS IT WERE. IT TYPI-FIES MY ATTITUDE TO LIFE, REALLY. IT'S ALL THERE, IT'S FUN, IT LOOKS GOOD, AND YOU DON'T HAVE TO WASH UP AFTERWARDS.

Molly Parkin
(1932 -)

171 McDonough Blvd.
SE Atlanta
404-627-9268
10:30a-8:30p Mon-Sat
No Plastic

and burgers ("charburgers," they call them), but these unquestionably take a back seat to the pork barbecue and the ribs. Tables are stocked with two sauces—one a thin, vinegar-based solution with a pretty high scorch factor, the other a thicker, sweeter potion recognizable by its snipped off cap. Or is it the other way around?

The side dishes pull their weight, especially the lightly dressed, sweet cole slaw and the Brunswick stew. Thick and meaty, it's brimming with corn and tomatoes and comes with three hunks of cornbread fairly teeming with pork cracklings (pig skin that's been fried crispy).

Barbecue is a notoriously labor-intensive proposition, and the guy in charge of chopping enough meat to satisfy the hungry hordes at

Harold's is no doubt on the fast track to carpal tunnel syndrome. There's definitely some artistry involved, though, and he works his magic right next to Harold's' answer to UV lamps: a small grill stoked with glowing embers, transferred by the shovelful from the barbecue pit. For dessert, neither of the homemade fried pies, peach or apple, will cause you a moment's regret. Should you appear overly anxious while waiting for these oil-bathed delights, the friendly waitresses will reassure you thusly: "Don't worry, hun, it's frying."

So LONG AS PEOPLE, BEING ILL-GOVERNED, SUFFER FROM HUNGER, CRIMINALS WILL NEVER DISAPPEAR.

Kenko Hoshi
The Harvest of Leisure
(c. 1330)

HAVANA SANDWICH SHOP

CUBAN

Those who think Fidel Castro has never done Americans any favors, consider this: were it not for the Bearded One's dictatorial ways, it's unlikely that Cuban sandwiches would have become such an alluring presence on the Atlanta dining scene. Over the years thousands of Cubanos have bolted their homeland for America, often aboard vessels of less than optimum buoyancy (the oars on the far wall are souvenirs from a successful flotilla). While that may be just the sort of thing to send Pat Buchanan into conniptions, any serious foodie sees it for the culinary windfall that it is.

Havana's hole-in-the-wall exterior, nicely accented by the hole-in-the-wall interior, belies a substantial, rock-solid menu. All sandwiches ($3-$4) are served on the same large and crusty loaves, leaving patrons the lone task of choosing a filling. The Cuban combines roast pork, ham, pickles and mojo sauce (an oil and vinegar dressing redolent with garlic and onions); tasty, no doubt, but better yet are the milanesa (breaded steak) and the boliche, sliced round steak prepared with green peppers and onions—cheese, too, if you like. To get the full Havana experience, root around for a bottle of habanero (alias "Scotch bonnet") sauce. Without peer among hot peppers, the wee habanero is long on flavor but not to be trifled with; start with a penny-sized puddle on your plate and dab your sandwich sparingly, lest you risk ruining a perfectly good pair of Dockers.

2905 Buford Highway
NE Atlanta
404-636-4094
10a-9:30p Mon-Sat
11a-7p Sun
No Plastic

Sandwiches aside, the daily specials are usually terrific and include yellow rice with either salad or the outstanding black beans (topped with sweet onions). Highlights include the beef stew, chicken granadina, and sturdy empanadas (fried pies filled beef or chicken). These last are best ordered only if you have a designated driver and can work a nap into the afternoon—they're on the heavy side. Among the beverages, there's no topping the dazzling selection of $1.75 batidos (the gringo term is "milkshakes"), featuring such tropical delights as papaya, mango and guanabana.

HEAPING BOWL AND BREW
SOUPS & STEWS

If you're wondering what Little Five Points looked like about 15 years ago, venture on over to East Atlanta, where a dose of urban renewal has spawned one of the city's grooviest eateries. With a thoroughly unpretentious decor and immense meals at giveaway prices, Heaping B & B has proved quite the magnet for those inclined toward serious eating.

Chief among the attractions are the Bowls, a remarkably broad array of cross-cultural concoctions whose only unifying theme is that they're piled into vessels large enough for bathing an infant. You know you've been living right when Ernest sets you up with a hearty helping of perogies (little dumplings filled with either mild sausage or potatoes and cheese, pan fried in butter and then slathered with sour cream). Other standouts include a comforting white bean chili, or basmati rice topped with Greens and Beans Stew (red and white

469 Flat Shoals Ave.
East Atlanta
404-523-8030
11:30a-3:30p,
5p-10p Mon-Thu
11:30a-3:30p,
5p-11p Fri
9:30a-11a Sat
V/MC

beans with collards and turnip greens in an earthy, herbed broth). All are served with a hearty slice of grilled sourdough.

Slightly lighter appetites may be well served by a dose of homemade soup—how does country ham with white beans and roasted red peppers strike you? They also do up respectable turkey burgers and a Mediterranean salad sandwich in a pita. As an accompaniment, the french-fried sweet potatoes, dusted with cinnamon pepper and served with a cranberry-mustard sauce, are nothing short of riveting.

As if that weren't enough, they pound away at your self-control with a pair of great desserts—chocolate bread pudding and a growth-stunting creation called Apple Crumble. Mindful of the effect all this gormandizing can have on even the most adroit eater, owner Todd Semrau has set up a little sitting area near the front door so you can regain your strength before hitting that long and dusty.

THEY CONSUMED THE WHOLE ANIMAL KINGDOM AT EACH MEAL.

George Bernard Shaw
(1856-1950)

HIMALAYA'S

INDIAN

Located across from Curry Honda—insert dumb joke here—in a large strip mall, Himalaya's is simply one of the best (and least expensive) Indian restaurants in the city. It is not, however, one of the better decorated, done up in a style that is best summarized as part Taj Mahal and part Amish barn-raising, with calico curtains separating the booths and the occasional pastoral woodcut placed among the Indian prints and photographs.

The food, however, is as authentic as it gets in these latitudes. To kick things off consider the

5520 PEACHTREE
INDUSTRIAL BLVD.
CHAMBLEE
770-458-6557
11:30A-2:30P,
5:30P-10P SUN-THU
11:30A-2:30P,
5:30P-10:30P FRI-SAT
V/MC/AMEX

samosas, though these can be pretty rich. The Mulligattawny soup is slightly less imposing and in every way delicious, a subtle intermingling of lentils, peas and onions in a sumptuous chicken broth.

While the combination meals—including soup, rice and clove-steeped tea—are the ticket at lunch, a la carte is the way it works at night. Their rendition of chicken tikka masala ($8) is splendid, smothered in a delicate and creamy sauce. The chicken makhani is a slightly milder variation, with a pronounced tomato presence. They also do a nice job with vindaloo (particularly the lamb), a vibrant dark curry spiced with cinnamon, coriander, and tamarind.

As is generally the case at Indian eateries, vegetarians have a number of rocking options ($5 or so), including a pair of potato dishes: the aloo gobi (spuds and cauliflower) and the aloo sag (potato and spinach). Though actually a side dish, the tarka dal (buttery lentils sprinkled with fried garlic) is another herbivore's delight. In appearance and texture it somewhat resembles hummus, and it mates up nicely with a puffy slat of fresh-baked naan.

HOLT BROS. BBQ

BARBECUE

After putting in their time on the corporate ladder—20 years with IBM and 16 with BellSouth, respectively—brothers Bill and James Holt decided they'd had it with the button-down life. They called it a career and went into the catering business, and in short order that enterprise evolved into a barbecue restaurant, housed in what was once a Hardee's burger outlet. If all that sounds

IF THE SPIT IS RIGHT, THEN THE MEAT IS RIGHT.

Indian proverb

6359 JIMMY CARTER BLVD.
NORCROSS
770-242-3984
11A-9P MON-THU
11A-10P FRI-SAT
12P-9P SUN
V/MC/AMEX

a little iffy, you're to be forgiven, but the fact is that in the course of finding entrepreneurial bliss these guys have become a reliable source for first-rate pork barbecue and homestyle vegetables.

If you come for lunch, $5 buys you a "Small" pork sandwich (don't let the name fool you), the obligatory Brunswick stew (loaded with barbecued chicken and pork), sweet cole slaw and a mound of skin-on french fries. At dinner, you'll do best with one of their plates, wherein cornbread and a trio of vegetables—the list typically includes fresh collards, fried okra and green beans—serve as spokes to a hub of smoked meats. In addition to the chopped pork, you'll also find pork ribs, beef brisket and turkey breast, all of which come up strong. Slightly less reliable are the Chicago-style hot links, which like everything else can be had as a solo sandwich.

In the event that you want to warm up before jumping headlong into a full meal, the cornmeal-crusted fried green tomatoes are the choice to make. Banish here and now any notions of getting the catfish nuggets, which are an unmitigated disrespecting of that frequently maligned fish. For lighter fare still adhering to the barbecue theme, try the chopped pork salad, a mound of meat atop a bed of iceberg lettuce. And for dessert, Cleo's sweet potato pie (made daily on the premises) should fulfill your needs and then some.

IN THE BOILING WATER THE FRANKFURTERS SWISHED AND LASHED LIKE ARTIFICIALLY COLORED AND MAGNIFIED PARAMECIA. IGNATIUS FILLED HIS LUNGS WITH THE PUNGENT, SOUR AROMA. "I SHALL PRETEND THAT I AM IN A SMART RESTAURANT AND THAT THIS IS THE LOBSTER POND."

John Kennedy Toole
A Confederacy of
Dunces (1980)

HONTO
CHINESE

3295 CHAMBLEE
DUNWOODY ROAD
CHAMBLEE
770-458-8088
11:30A-9:45P
SUN-THU
11:30A-10:45P
FRI-SAT
V/MC/AMEX

Situated smack in the heart of Chamblee's Chinatown, Honto is one of the more authentic and comprehensive Chinese eateries in all of greater Atlanta. Given the location, it's little surprise that the place is routinely packed, especially at lunch. Unless they know you—particularly if you don't look Chinese, or at least Asian—they'll probably hand you the Americanized Chinese menu, packed with all the familiar lo meins, foo youngs, and so forth. If this is what you get, hand it back and ask for the far more interesting Hong Kong menu. In characteristic Cantonese/Southern Chinese style, both are of Tolstoyian dimensions in terms of length.

The Hong Kong bill of fare is heavy on the seafood. If you're feeling flush enough in the pocketbook not to be deterred by the term "market price," the Maine lobster with ginger and scallion or black bean sauce will leave you smiling, as will the pan-fried whole pompano and the garlicky jumbo prawns (served heads and all). If you're more interested in nonaquatic (and cheaper) entrees, the steamed spare ribs with black bean sauce and the Salt and Pepper Crispy Chicken are excellent. The Buddha Delight rates tops among the vegetarian options. The soups are also well done, led by the slightly bitter mustard green version and the shredded pork and duck meat combo.

If you do end up casting your lot with the American menu, stick with the chef's specials, particularly the sizzling Happy Family (damn near

NOWADAYS, CHINESE PEOPLE TEND TO EAT TOO MUCH. BESIDES FEEDING THEMSELVES THEY LIKE TO LOOK AT A LOT OF FOOD. HOW CAN IT PLEASE THEM TO LOUNGE ABOUT ALL DAY FOR THE SAKE OF SOME DELICACIES, SOILING THEIR MOUTHS WITH ROASTS AND SMOKED MEATS?

Anonymous
(c. 350 A.D.)

every kind of meat and seafood you can name, along with a few vegetables), or the distinctive seafood wor ba (lobster, crab, shrimp, and scallops in a thin, tomatoey sauce served over crispy rice patties). They also put on a pretty high-caliber dim sum spread every day, and it's even more elaborate on the weekends. Take note that, while it officially runs into the early afternoon, the list of offerings grows pretty thin by noon or so.

Hot Pepper Thai

THAI

Though the atmosphere here is subdued and relaxing—floral wallpaper, linen tablecloths, peaceful music—the food is anything but tame. Seemingly irrespective of who's in charge of the wok, chile peppers get tossed around like they were candy. Dishes you might order hot or medium at other restaurants are best gotten mild here, as anything medium or above is liable to cause physical pain. Utter the phrase "I'd like that hot" and the gloves come off entirely.

2257 Lenox Road
NE Atlanta
404-634-1784
11:30a-2:30p,
5:30p-10:30p Mon-Thu
11:30a-2:30p,
5:30p-11:30p Fri
5:30p-11:30p Sat
5:30p-10:30p Sun
V/MC/AMEX

Lunch specials include a so-so spring roll and a satisfying bowl of one of the world's finer soups, tom kha gai. Made with coconut milk, it's flavored with bits of chicken, lemongrass, cilantro, and those pleasantly bulbous little straw mushrooms. Tops among the midday entrees are the spicy catfish—a far more common sight at Vietnamese restaurants—and the crispy Bangkok duck, a sweet bargain at $5.25. If you dig noodle dishes, any version of the pad thai is worth getting, as are the beef drunken noodles, doused with a dark, gingery gravy.

If you're coming to sup, prices take a slight jump to the $6-$7 range. If you fancy an appetizer, the mussels are the one to get, delicately steamed with lemongrass and basil and served with chile sauce. In addition to the aforementioned roasted duck, they also do up a sauteed version, which is kept company by sweet red peppers and a fistful of Thai basil (more of a licorice taste to it than Italian basil). The salmon curry is also a nice way to go, and it's milder than the majority of offerings.

Set back from the road at a 45-degree angle, this single-story building is long and thin, with tables running along each wall. The interior has a feel not unlike that of an Amtrak dining car. Or an unusually fancy single-wide mobile home. In any event, this odd layout makes for some very dimly lit tables along the back wall, which you can either specifically request or avoid as you see fit.

JALISCO
MEXICAN

After feeding your head poring over the incredible selection of used readables at the nearby Oxford Books Too, you can satiate your belly by trotting down the hill to this Mexican eatery. Whatever the stark interior lacks in terms of character (everything) is more than compensated for by the friendly staff (particularly accommodating of families with young children) and some truly wondrous soups.

THE SPEED WITH WHICH HOT PEPPERS SPREAD AROUND THE GLOBE IS UNEQUALLED IN THE ANNALS OF FOOD.

Richard Schweid
Hot Peppers (1980)

2337 PEACHTREE ROAD
BUCKHEAD
404-261-8971
11A-2:30P,
5P-10:30P MON-FRI
12P-10:30P SAT
AMEX

They start you off right with some excellent chips (served warm) and a mild salsa that's jammed with cilantro. Of the aforementioned soups, none is more fetching than the colorful Mexican stew, its delicate stock teeming with chopped steak, jalapenos, onions, tomatoes and chilled avocado chunks.

A sidecar of lime is provided so you can squeeze a few drops into the mix just prior to wading in. It's beautiful stuff, and the same loving attention is administered to the chicken soup (white and dark meat with hunks of celery, carrots, pungent white onions and slices of mild poblano peppers), and the bean version (chicken broth with pintos cooked to the point of dissolving, flavored with fresh cilantro and green onions).

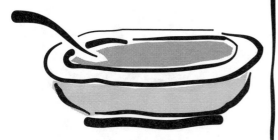

The cheap combinations at lunch (all around $4) consist of a solid selection of burritos, tacos, enchiladas and chalupas. For supper, skip the combos and order from the list of house specialties most of which are in the $8 range). The carnitas dinner is particularly tasty: grilled pork tips served with salad, beans and their splendid rice (light, fluffy and chock full of potatoes). Unless you have a singular fondness for bright orange liquid cheese, steer clear of the Mexican hamburger, which is about as strong a candidate for deportation as you'll find.

I WOULD RATHER STUFF MYSELF WITH GAZ- PACHOS THAN BE SUBJECT TO THE MIS- ERY OF AN IMPERTINENT PHYSICIAN WHO KILLS ME WITH HUNGER.

Miguel de Cervantes
Don Quixote (1605-15)

JAVA JIVE
COFFEEHOUSE

790 PONCE DE LEON AVE.
PONCEY-HIGHLANDS
404-876-6161
8A-2P, 6P-12A TUE-FRI
10A-2:30P, 6P-12A SAT
10A-2:30P SUN
NO PLASTIC

Agent Cooper was fond of referring to the mythical town of Twin Peaks as a place where you could get a decent cup of coffee and a damn good piece of pie. That description could neatly describe Java Jive, a coffeehouse masquerading as an American kitchen, circa 1959. Few among us lament the passing of bright vinyl and formica dinette sets from the landscape, but their presence here, along

with a barrage of Benny Goodman tunes, is quite the kick and seems to foster good vibes and plenty of banter.

The retro theme does not extend to the coffees, which thankfully bear no resemblance to the percolated swill of the Java Dark Ages. Nope, the Jivers come across with a solid roster of caffeinated beverages, most of them espresso-based. They are all to be trusted with the exception of the Moccachino, docked big points for its halo of Reddi-Wip—any ersatz dairy product that comes in a container marked "WARNING: Do Not Incinerate" has no business in a coffee cup. Among the raft of baked goods (all in the $3 range) you'll want to seek out the pecan pie, with its oozy center and crunchy top, and the alarmingly dense chocolate swirl cheesecake. If you like ice cream, check out the $4 Shot 'N Shake (your choice of milkshake spiked with espresso), and the equally rich Coffee Float—a scoop of chocolate or vanilla bobbing in a glass of regular brew.

If you want an actual meal, they've recently added a menu that recalls the same era as the furniture—think meatloaf, or center-cut pork chops with glazed apples—and is generally quite respectable. The one major exception is the Tofu Scramble, seemingly a product of the school that views vegetarian dining as a spice-deprived form of punishment. It rates as perhaps the most curious tool of penance since the hairshirt, and is to be indulged in only on those terms.

JERSEY'S
AUTHENTIC SUBS
SANDWICHES

Unless you've hunkered down with a sub sandwich north of the Mason-Dixon line, chances are you've settled for cheap imitations of a true, overstuffed grinder. Though the majority of Hotlanta's subs are pitifully small and uninteresting, the city is graced with a few transplanted purveyors of decent hoagies. Jersey's are the real deal, qualitywise, and large enough to put you in mind of a Christo

4920 ROSWELL ROAD
SANDY SPRINGS
404-847-0576
11A-8P MON-FRI
11A-7P SAT
NO PLASTIC

art project—unless you have oversized mitts, you'll have to cradle the roll with both hands.

The small eat-in area can seem a mite frantic round about lunchtime. At the center of the action is owner Ken Celmer, pounding the register keys and making sure you get what you need, be it a diet Snapple or one of those bigass kosher dills.

He'll also answer any sandwich questions, though the large menu board pretty well spells out the options: about 20 cold and hot subs, combining most any of the standard meats (roast beef, turkey, boiled ham, and so on) and cheeses (swiss, provolone, cheddar, blah blah) on a huge freshly baked roll for around $4.

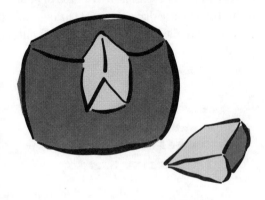

For about a buck more, there's also a roster of specialty sandwiches, led by the superb grilled Reuben and the marinated chicken breast club. Finally, Jersey's cheese steaks—a hearty melding of white American cheese (that's right, *American* cheese) onions, green peppers and sliced flank steak—are as good as any in town and filling enough to have your lids drooping and your speech slurring. If you can't make it to Pat's in Philadelphia, this is about as close as it comes.

NEVER COMMIT YOUR-
SELF TO A CHEESE
WITHOUT HAVING
FIRST EXAMINED IT.

T.S. Eliot
(1888-1965)

JOE'S TO GOES
BURGERS

A decidedly juvenile attitude prevails here, blaringly apparent in everything from the chirping video games to their implicit invitiation to revisit your formative years and write on the walls. In fact, they even provide fresh Sharpies, with which corny limericks are inscribed, teen crushes professed, and more than a few unflattering references to Rush Limbaugh's girth writ large. Not coincidentally, takeout is popular, and there's a separate area dedicated to that pursuit.

While not exactly breaking new ground in terms of cuisine, Joe's quintessentially American menu doesn't put on any airs. The half-pound, hand-patted burgers are top-notch and come fully dressed (as does the waitstaff, thank god), with a side of thick home fries. On down the list you'll find chicken wings, hot dogs, cheese steaks and barbecued short ribs. These last are quite the treat, tiny and tender little guys that run $8 for a one-pound order. Otherwise most everything is five bucks or less.

All of the side items—baked beans, cole slaw, and similar ilk—are made fresh on the premises and generally very fine. The familiar fried goodies that enjoy a certain omnipresence in American taverns—cheese sticks, chicken fingers, and the latest craze, jalapeno poppers—are all decent, if not exactly featherlight. While you're waiting, amble over to the free jukebox and override the house stereo that's blaring Foghat and Bad Company with the likes of Frankie Lymon or The O'Jays. To cut

2880 Holcomb Bridge Road
Alpharetta
770-552-9855

4051 Highway 78 SW
Lilburn
770-985-2035

605 Indian Trail-Lilburn Road
Lilburn
770-931-3001

4842 Redan Road
Stone Mountain
404-296-5637

11a-11p Mon-Thu
11a-12a Fri-Sat
12p-10p Sun
V/MC

Dining-out is a vice, a dissipation of spirit punished by remorse.

Cyril Connolly
The Unquiet Grave
(1944)

the road dust, you have your choice from all manner of American lagers (they're pushing quantity, not necessarily quality), fountain sodas, iced tea and bottled IBC root beer. For dessert, pay your bill and head elsewhere.

JONATHAN LEE'S
CHINESE & THAI

1799 BRIARCLIFF ROAD
EMORY AREA
404-897-1700
11A-10P SUN-THU
11A-11P FRI-SAT
V/MC/AMEX

Although the 20-foot ceilings impart a sort of a National Guard Armory ambience, Jonathan Lee's is home to some elegant Asian eats. They deftly manage the often dicey task of mixing cuisines, offering a wide assortment of skillfully prepared Chinese dishes intermingled with a distinguished slate of Thai prospects.

Among the preliminary courses, the nod goes to the Thai appetizers. The beef ribs and the marinated chicken satay with peanut sauce are strong choices. Regardless of heritage, any of the 10 soups will do you right, though the creamy chicken with corn and the tom yum (a racy Thai concoction) are perhaps the best.

WHEN THE SUN RISES
I GO TO WORK,

WHEN THE SUN GOES
DOWN, I TAKE MY
REST,

I DIG THE WELL FROM
WHICH I DRINK,

I FARM THE SOIL THAT
YIELDS MY FOOD,

I SHARE CREATION.
KINGS CAN DO NO
MORE.

Unknown Chinese
author
(2500 B.C.)

Entrees of note range from a straightforward chicken curry to Princess Nails—didn't I see her wrestle at the Omni?—which are peppery chicken wings stuffed with bamboo shoots, mushrooms and water chestnuts. Topping the list of seafood dishes are the garlic scallops and the Cupid Prawns, frolicking in a coconut cream sauce flecked with cilantro. Vegetarians are well provided for, with the eggplant and black mushrooms in a puckery garlic sauce or the stir-fried Chinese cabbage, likewise heavy on the garlic with a scraping of fresh ginger. Both are under $7.

Portions are large enough that you'll likely end up strutting out with a doggie bag, especially if you're looking to get busy with one of Jonathan's category-defying desserts. Cast your lot with either the Pineapple Heaven (deep-fried pineapple bits atop coconut ice cream, spiked with orange liqueur) or the Mount Fuji—a sort of Baked Alaska derivative, featuring ice cream capped with meringue and "flambeed into an erupting volcano of pleasure." Sounds like something you might see advertised in Times Square, but it's my-T fine.

KIM TIN
INDONESIAN

As a main stop on the Europe-to-Asia trade route, the Indonesian archipelago has, over the centuries, been profoundly influenced by a bevy of cultures, most notably Indian, Thai and Chinese. The resulting cuisine—a zesty conglomeration of curries, chile peppers and seafood artistry—reflects the complexity of the country itself, and as a result it's not the sort of thing that fares too well in the hands of non-native chefs.

Kim Tin is Atlanta's sole purveyor of Indonesian eats, and a compelling Southeast Asian alternative in a town where Thai restaurants continue to proliferate like goldfish. Though they have some Thai and Chinese dishes, these are reserved mainly for skeptics; the 14 Indonesian offerings are the main draw, and that's the direction to be looking. From the rendang (beef cooked in curry and coconut milk) and the scorching kari ayam (chicken and potatoes) to the squid and snapper selections ($9 or so), experimentation yields substantial rewards.

4646-A BUFORD HIGHWAY
CHAMBLEE
770-454-0555
11:30A-10P MON-FRI
12P-10P SAT-SUN
V/MC/AMEX

If you're looking to do some serious firewalking, both the soto ayam and the soto sapi (containing chicken and beef, respectively) are simmered in coconut milk and topped with a blistering chili-lime sauce. For something more subtle, keep an eye out for the peach chicken (lightly fried filets in a thick, sweet sauce with tomatoes, peaches and green peppers), which is only offered when they can get good fruit. For noodle fans, mei rebus is the way to go, served in a huge bowl with celery, potatoes and bean sprouts. To complete the picture, there is no more intriguing a beverage than the Indo es campur—red beans, coconut cream, palm seeds and jelly, served over ice.

KOOL KORNER
CUBAN SANDWICHES

Georgia Tech students and Armani-clad Midtown business folk will be the first to rave about Kool Korner and the last to give you directions. Regulars seem to take a proprietary interest in this teeny grocery, which manages to draw a crowd based solely on the strength of the Cuban sandwiches. Despite the fact that it lacks a telephone, a real sign and even so much as a single parking space, it's not uncommon to get caught in a a 20-person line.

Perched behind a head-high shield of plexiglass—c'mon now, what's a restaurant without one?—the proprietor stacks up roast pork, ham, onions and jalapeno peppers like a skilled mason, ably assisted by one or two young women who's job it is to chop what needs chopping and grill what needs grilling.

DO I DARE TO EAT A PEACH?

T.S. Eliot
The Love Song of J.
Alfred Prufrock (1915)

349 14TH ST.
MIDTOWN
404-892-4424
10:30A-6P MON-FRI
12P-5P SAT
NO PLASTIC

Approaching his task with a focus that would be the envy of any diamond cutter, the sandwich master is usually oblivious to the hungry horde's prompts and questions. If he wants to hear from you he'll let you know—usually by the time you're fourth or so in line, so be ready. When your time comes, be mindful that complicated orders have a tendency to get bungled, so don't be too surprised if you get a pile of jalapenos when you requested double onions.

If you've ever said to yourself, "I wonder what it's like shopping in Havana?," the sparse shelves at Kool Korner are probably a close approximation. Sodas, a little fresh fruit, bags of plantain chips and not much else. Meanwhile, the lunchtime feeding frenzy usually doesn't subside until they run out of the requisite flat loaves of bread, at which time the maestro takes a bow and retires to the back room.

LAWRENCE'S CAFE
MIDDLE EASTERN

For a one-stop, night-on-the-town Atlanta dining experience complete with live entertainment, you'd be right in expecting to foot a premium tab. Not so at Lawrence's Cafe, where the fine Middle Eastern cuisine is served amid dark and cozy confines punctuated by undulating belly dancers. The atmosphere is further enhanced by a large oil painting of the restaurant's beturbaned namesake, adventurer T.E. Lawrence—better known as Lawrence of Arabia.

The lunch menu tops out at about six bucks, and you can feast on platters of gyros, kabobs and

IT IS SHEER FOOL-HARDINESS TO BE ARROGANT TO A COOK.

Agnes Repplier
Americans and Others
(1912)

2888 BUFORD HIGHWAY
NE ATLANTA
404-320-7756
11A-3P, 5P-10P
MON-THU
11A-11P FRI
12P-3P, 5P-11P SAT
V/MC/AMEX

sliced leg of lamb, as well as a couscous-based stew loaded with beef, chicken and vegetables. All meals are accompanied by excellent tabouli salad (a conglomeration of bulgar wheat, parsley, tomatoes, onions, mint, olive oil and lemon juice). Some also come with a sizeable dollop of terrific hummus, drizzled with olive oil, dusted with paprika and fairly begging to be scooped up with a hunk of pita. Speaking of pita, they do up a baked Pita Pizza, topped with hummus, feta cheese, fresh tomatoes and a meat of your choosing (the lamb works well). A little on the gimmicky side, perhaps, but nonetheless a satisfying twist for the tastebuds.

Even with the floor show, you can easily eat dinner for under $12 (excluding drinks, mind you). The expanded evening menu includes shish taook (marinated chicken and vegetables), samboosk (delicate phyllo-like pastry stuffed with ground meat and nuts, served with yogurt) and stuffed grape leaves. If you've got a taste for fowl, opt for the quail—two birds sauteed in white wine and garlic oil. Top off the evening with a cup of chamomile tea or their paint-thick Turkish coffee, and make sure you take care of Coco as she jingles past.

MACHU PICCHU
PERUVIAN

3375 Buford Highway NE Atlanta
404-320-3226
11a-11p Daily
V/MC/AMEX

Though the hole-in-the-mall location, with its prefab interior and cliched Peruvian decorations—enough already with the llama photos—is nothing to go e-mailing home about, the staff here is exceedingly friendly and the Andean delights they serve up are the most authentic you'll find this side of Lake Titicaca. Not that Peruvian eateries are exactly one to a block in this part of the world, but as you'll discover that has more to do with the remoteness of the country than any deficiencies of its cuisine.

Non-Spanish-speakers should definitely track down one of the bilingual menus, lest they find themselves inadvertently staring down one of the house specialties—a sizzling anticucho (beef heart kabob). Skewered organ meats aside, the list of offerings represent an amalgamation of influences, most notably that of the Spanish, who dropped in on the Incas and hung around for several centuries

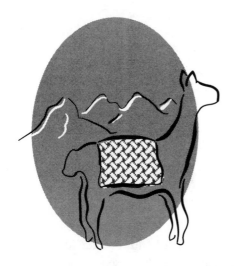

before bugging out in the early 1800s. Though it's tempting to draw analogies with Mexican food, one can fairly easily overstate the similarities. Both favor corn and chile peppers, but Peruvians also carry on a rather torrid love affair with the potato, which you'll find in several dishes here.

Peru's attenuated coastline means seafood figures prominently in the native cuisine. Of the four shrimp dishes, the picante de camarones (simmered in a chunky salsa) is especially good but not for the faint of palate. If you're aching for other

I NOW DISMISS THE POTATO WITH THE HOPE THAT I SHALL NEVER AGAIN HAVE TO WRITE THE WORD, OR SEE THE THING.

William Cobbett
A Year's Residence in the United States of America (1819)

denizens of the deep, forego the fried fish entrees in favor of the $5-range seafood ceviches, which are marinated in lemon juice and served cold.

Most of the beef and chicken dishes (nothing over $6) are prepared identically—bistek apanado (breaded steak served with rice and a salad) is an especially auspicious option. With each meal, you get a crusty little loaf of bread, the idea being for you to dip hunks of it in an orange-tinted chile sauce. The dessert of choice is a barely sweet purple rice pudding.

MADRAS CAFE
INDIAN

3086 BRIARCLIFF ROAD
NE ATLANTA
404-320-7120
11:30A-3P
5:30P-8:30P MON-FRI
12P-8:30P SAT-SUN
NO PLASTIC

This little 10-table family joint in the Williamsburg Village shopping complex bills its chow as a sort of Indian fast food. That's accurate enough as far as it goes, given the fact that you can get a lot of satisfying fried stuff at unbelievably cheap prices, but there ends the somewhat unflattering association with the American notion of fast food. Exit the pimply teen cashier and the squawk of a malfunctioning intercom; enter a berobed, bearded gentleman and the soothing twang of a sitar.

Places like Madras Cafe go a long way toward helping even the most devoted carnivore understand how vegetarians can live the meatless life without feeling as though they're missing out. The story here is more one of quality than selection; the two standard specials are your primary choices, both very tasty and available all day. One comes with rice, naan, vegetables in a curry sauce and a tiny dish of raita (their's is a yogurt and cucumber combo) for $3.50. The other option is a buck more and comes with sambar (a thick lentil soup), a pair of idlis (steamed rice cakes), some killer coconut chutney, and a masala dhosai (sometimes called a dosa, it's a crispy-edged crepe about the size of a bath mat, filled with onions and potatoes).

You can also cobble together a meal from the a la carte menu, in which case you'll want to know about the uthappam (an unleavened griddle bread topped with onions, chiles and cilantro), the medhu vadai (deep-fried lentil patties) and the tried-and-true vegetable samosas. For about a dollar you can choose from six desserts, ranging from the doughnut-like jilebi to carrot halwa (shredded boiled carrots in milk with sugar and butter). Common to them all is a sweetness quotient that's nearly off the scale. Service is quick and friendly, and you clear your own styrofoam plates when you're finished.

Majestic Food Shop
CLASSIC DINER

The Majestic first opened for business in 1929, just as Wall Street was going in the dumper in a big way. Not exactly the ideal time to launch a small business, but nonetheless this unassuming diner has endured lo these many years. What's more, while the mind boggles at the changes that have occurred around this Poncey-Highlands landmark over the decades, it still looks much the way it did during the Depression. With chrome counter

1031 PONCE DE LEON AVE.
PONCEY-HIGHLANDS
404-875-0276
OPEN 24 HOURS
NO PLASTIC

stools, thick institutional china, and a Social-Security-office-green color scheme, it seems like something lifted from an Edward Hopper painting.

Foodwise, as you might well imagine, they don't exactly go chasing every trend to come down the pike. The menu is slam full of cheap and substantial diner favorites, things like sturdy cheeseburgers (with thick-cut fries, $3) and club sandwiches on toasted white bread. If you want to get to working the silverware, they'll throw a T-bone on the grill and serve it up with a hefty Idaho spud for $8.

Breakfast is, of course, also a big draw; once again, the selections are hardly what you would call exotic, revolving around an axis of flapjacks, eggs and bacon. Frosted Flakes in those little single-serving boxes are about as racy as it gets. The coffee is, well, coffee.

If you're capping off a meal or dropping in after a movie, the apple and cherry pies—what were you expecting?—are a point of considerable pride. Though they often possess the overtly friendly veneer that non-Southerners seem to expect when in Dixie, the world-weary waitresses are more than willing to go easy on the chit-chat if you are.

MALAYSIA HOUSE
MALAYSIAN

It's one of the burning questions of the nineties: can a mom-and-pop Asian eatery peacefully coexist alongside a heavily capitalized chain restaurant offering bosomy waitresses and forgettable chicken wings? For Malaysia House's Burmese predecessor, Mandalay, the answer was no; after trying to make a go of it in the same strip shopping center that is home to a Hooter's, they closed up shop in 1995. In its place, however, has emerged an equally alluring prospect, the city's only source for true Malaysian cuisine. Cross your fingers.

If this place does end up taking the gaspipe, rest assured it won't be because of the food. The charcoal grilled satay (skewered morsels of beef or chicken) are a beautiful way to kick things off. They're served with a little dish of sliced cucumber and onion, along with densely packed rice squares and a bowl of thin peanut sauce for dipping.

Heading the entrees are seafood dishes like Assam Shrimp (shelled and served in a red pepper and tamarind sauce), and the Sauced Squid (simmered in a bath of soy, garlic, ginger and scallions). The curry dishes are also worthwhile, specifically the boneless chicken version, rich with potatoes and coconut milk, and the Curry Vegetarian ($8.95), stocked with baby corn, snow peas, mushrooms and thinly sliced carrots. Chile peppers are in evidence throughout the menu, and you can be sure that any dish specifically denoted as spicy will be that and more. Flaming tongues can be nicely extinguished by a dish of homemade coconut ice cream ($1.50).

5945 JIMMY CARTER BLVD.
NORCROSS
770-368-8368
11:30A-3P, 5:30P-10P
MON, WED & THU
11:30A-3P,
5:30P-10:30P FRI
12P-3P, 5:30P-10:30P
SAT-SUN
V/MC/AMEX

GO AS A MEAT PIE, COME BACK AS A SANDWICH.

Malaysian proverb

MAMBO

CUBAN

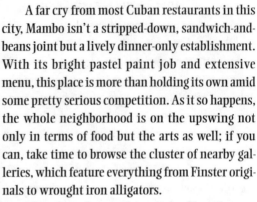

1402-8 NORTH
HIGHLAND AVE.
MORNINGSIDE
404-876-2626
5:30P-12A DAILY
V/MC/AMEX

A far cry from most Cuban restaurants in this city, Mambo isn't a stripped-down, sandwich-and-beans joint but a lively dinner-only establishment. With its bright pastel paint job and extensive menu, this place is more than holding its own amid some pretty serious competition. As it so happens, the whole neighborhood is on the upswing not only in terms of food but the arts as well; if you can, take time to browse the cluster of nearby galleries, which feature everything from Finster originals to wrought iron alligators.

The atmosphere is characterized by salsa music, an autographed photo of Desi Arnaz, and, on the weekends, throngs of people. Once you're seated (in the main dining room or at one of the sidewalk tables) you'll get plenty of quality time from the knowledgeable waitstaff. They'll likely advise an appetizer, best of which are the fresh mussels (sauteed with onions, sweet peppers, tomatoes and olives, $5.25) and a mouth-watering knob of goat cheese baked in a tomato and olive sauce. Soup makes for another fine leadoff, either the fiery black bean, or, if they have it, the winter gazpacho (served warm).

If you're of a traditional mind, opt for either the picadillo (chopped sirloin sauteed with onions and green peppers and topped with olives and raisins) or puerco asado (roasted pork marinated in lime and garlic-infested mojo sauce). These run in the $7-$9 range and include black beans and rice. Paella lovers will find two versions of that Spanish mainstay, either with seafood (whatever's fresh) nestled amid saffron rice, chicken and chorizo, or the vegetarian alternative (artichoke hearts, black olives, zucchini, mushrooms, sweet peppers and onions).

The daily fish special (usually red snapper or grouper marinated in garlic and olive oil) is a tad spendy ($15 or so), but usually excellent, prepared to order (pan-fried, baked or grilled) with the head and tail left on for dramatic purposes. The menu is rounded out by the obligatory Cuban sandwich and a squadron of salads, headed by the excellent Mediterranean: Bibb lettuce topped with white beans, tomatoes, red onions, manchego cheese, olive oil and balsamic vinegar.

MARY MAC'S TEA ROOM
MEAT-&-THREE

Time stands still at Mary Mac's, one of the city's most celebrated restaurants and the first place cabbies take out-of-towners when bucking for a sizeable gratuity. Since war widow and founder Mary McKenzie first strung on her apron in 1945, the place has quadrupled in size—thanks mainly to the entrepreneurial acumen of second owner Margaret Lupo—yet the genteel atmosphere and skillful cooking remain uncompromised.

If you haven't heard, Mary Mac's fried chicken has long been lauded as among the best around. While the accolades are deserved, the kitchen crew are hardly one-trick ponies in the down-home entree department; every bit as attractive are the chicken and dumplings, country-fried steak,

224 Ponce de Leon Ave.
Midtown
404-876-1800
11a-9p Mon-Fri
9a-9p Sat
9a-3p Sun
No Plastic

ketchup-glazed meatloaf and the Chicken Pan Pie (like traditional chicken pot pie, minus the vegetables). Whatever your choice, a meat and three vegetables with an assortment of hot breads will run you just over $7.

Regarding the vegetables, the hot items are often exquisite, the cold offerings strictly minor league. Among the 20 or so viable possibilities are a couple of rarely seen Southern gems, namely pot likker—salty collard broth, served with a sweet yellow corn muffin—and hopping John, a blend of black-eyed peas, rice and hock meat. The latter appears as part of a rotating menu of side dishes, which changes with the seasons. Others to look for are the tiny field peas and the honey-baked onions.

Though they have a full bar, every Southerner knows that cocktails and collard greens mesh about as well as Pat Sajak and Howard Stern. The one, the only way to get the full Mary Mac's effect is with an icy glass of sweet tea. You'll find the servers to be some of the friendliest anywhere, true Southern belles who pronounce the "L" in salmon with an almost giddy exaggeration. To cap off your meal, watch for the coconut cake or banana pudding; the unquestioned star, though, is the peach cobbler, with its thick, buttery crust.

MATTHEWS CAFETERIA

MEAT-&-THREE

On weekdays, if you arrive at Matthews after 11:30 a.m. the gravel parking lot will likely be filled with pickup trucks. Contractors are mad for the place, and they routinely combine a visit to Cofer Building Supply across the street with a heavy-duty, Southern-style cafeteria meal. Don't get all slack-jawed and whiney, however, if you find yourself anchoring a line that curls through a sea of red-checkered tablecloths; decades of success have taught these folks how to handle crowds—not only is the service snappy and no-nonsense, but they've crammed tables into nearly every square inch of the building.

Gliding your plastic tray along the waist-high metal shelf, you'll come first upon a slew of salads (things like grated carrots with raisins, and all manner of fruit-filled, Jello-based concoctions) and desserts (the banana pudding is incredible, most of the others are hit-and-miss). Next up are the entrees, which vary on a daily basis. Though the quality level is uniformly high, they do an especially fine job with meatloaf, turkey and dressing (chunky-style cornbread stuffing with onions and celery) and, believe it or don't, liver and onions. Obviously, this one either speaks to you or it

2299 MAIN ST.
TUCKER
770-491-9577
10:45A-3P, 4:30P-8P
DAILY
NO PLASTIC

doesn't, but if you're of the habit, you won't be disappointed. The entrees usually cost about $2.50, and for an extra buck you can get a double order.

As far as gravy sopping is concerned, both the yeasty dinner rolls and the firm but moist yellow cornbread come up strong. Veggiewise, everything's fresh as all get-out—sweet corn on the cob with bits of husk and silk still clinging; green beans seasoned with hamhock, great mashed potatoes. On occasion they offer a terrific baked casserole made with cheddar cheese, Vidalia onion and eggs; not unlike a rectangular quiche, though lord knows you'll never hear that term crossing their lips. Just about everything runs 85 cents a throw, and sliced tomatoes, sweet Vidalias and whole scallions are also available for a nominal charge. During the summer, much of what you see is plucked fresh from the sizeable garden out back.

THE MEAN BEAN
TEX-MEX

Mexican eateries run by non-Mexicans are often a shaky proposition at best, but the Mean Bean manages to turn the trick quite nicely. Never mind that the by-gringos-for-gringos menu is far less likely to fill the bill for a homesick Juan Q. Public than, say, a lifetime subscriber to *Mother Jones*; their emphasis on quality ingredients and value for money are worth knowing about, and have found an adoring audience both here in Little Five Points and in Athens, a few blocks from the UGA campus.

Orders are placed at the back counter. The selection includes burritos, quesadillas, enchiladas, tacos, chili and a few salads. Burritos are especially

453 MORELAND AVE.
LITTLE FIVE POINTS
770-525-0062
11:30A-10P MON-THU
11:30A-11P FRI-SAT
11:30A-10P SUN
NO PLASTIC

well done, wrapped in huge flour tortillas that have been prepped with a chunky red salsa and grated jack cheese. Best of the lot is the chicken, Spanish rice and spinach combo, and at $4 and change this gutbuster is the priciest thing on the menu. Though it would have them scratching their heads down Guadalajara way, the chili is another standout—it's a steamy morass of pinto beans, bulgar wheat, green peppers, celery, carrots, onions and tomatoes. With either shredded beef or chicken it still checks in under $3.50.

The drink cooler is to your right, and there you'll find the requisite sodas as well as a disturbing quantity of tangerine Fruitopia. If you're looking to work a little malt into the mix, have 'em draw you a draft of Shiner Bock, Honey Brown or New Amsterdam.

HUNGER AND RECENT ILL-USAGE ARE GREAT ASSISTANTS IF YOU WANT TO CRY.

Charles Dickens
Oliver Twist (1837-38)

While waiting for your chow you can groove to the likes of Jethro Tull or Nirvana, or sift through the toy basket. The knickknacks therein harken to decades previous, things like Duncan yo-yos and a stuffed Rocky the Flying Squirrel. Keep your wits about you, though, until your order comes up—the pony-tailed kitchen crew doesn't suffer slowpokes gladly, and they're apt to glare menacingly if they have to call you more than twice.

MEXICO CITY GOURMET

MEXICAN

2134 N. DECATUR ROAD
EMORY AREA
404-634-1128

5500 CHAMBLEE-
DUNWOODY ROAD
DUNWOODY
770-396-1111

10:30A-10P MON-FRI
10:30A-11P SAT-SUN
V/MC/AMEX

With all the hokey Mexican eateries blighting the landscape these days, locating one with any real merit can be like trying to find a women's bathroom at the Citadel. Mexico City Gourmet stands above the throng of pretenders with a rousing mix of creatively prepared dishes, colossal portions and friendly service.

Specialties of the house include what may well be the city's finest chile relleno (a roasted poblano pepper bulging with ground beef, almonds, raisins and spices); a grilled ribeye taco topped with onions, mushrooms and chopped poblanos; and the chicken or steak rancheros, which come smothered in an amalgam of jalapenos, tomatoes and cilantro that's both attractive and hot enough to leave your tongue feeling like the business end of a tiki torch. Prices hover in the $6-$9 range.

Two cold seafood salads (both around $6, served with avocado wedges) are also particularly scrumptious—the ceviche (lemon-marinated hunks of red snapper) and the shrimp and scallop scabeche (large portions of each marinated in a heady bath of lemon juice, onions, olive oil and jalapeno). If you have a hankering for soup, the jalapeno-bean—pintos in a rich stock churning with bacon, cilantro, onion, tomato and hot peppers—is the surest bet to come along since Shaq went hardship. Cap your visit with homemade flan (topped with whipped cream and Kahlua upon request) or an artfully arranged heap of sopapillas

THE BELLY RULES THE MIND.

Spanish proverb

topped with cinnamon and sugar. Among the potables, a chilly margarita (rocks or frozen) or pitcher of sangria are available to take away your pain.

As for atmosphere, the haphazard collection of posters and wall-mounted trinkets add a homey feel to the diminutive original dining room (they've since added a bar and extra seating). In the evenings they sometimes have live music at the Decatur Road location, usually American lounge standards crooned by a fellow accompanying himself on guitar. Joao Gilberto he ain't, but he knows a lick or two.

MOCHA
COFFEEHOUSE

As coffeehouses continue to spring up around Atlanta after every big rain, MOCHA is one of the early arrivals still holding its own in a hopelessly crowded field. Though the atmosphere is pleasant enough—moody, synthesizer music and rotating exhibits of humorous artworks, including the political cartoons of homegrown Pulitzer Prize winners Doug Marlette and Mike Luckovich—and the coffee quite respectable, these don't exactly set them apart from the competition. What does, however, especially when the mercury gets to creeping upward, are their excellent ice creams and sorbets.

As you enter, the coffee area is to your right, with an extensive list of javas of the day. The frozen stuff, meanwhile, can be found down at the

1424 N. HIGHLAND AVE.
MORNINGSIDE
404-881-8008
7:30A-10:30P
TUE-THU
7:30A-12A FRI
8A-12A SAT
10A-11P SUN
V/MC

other end of this narrow space. Naturally enough, coffee ice cream is a perennial choice, along with vanilla, strawberry and the occasional other berry. If you're after sorbet, they usually have one or more excellent citrus flavors. Servings are a buck and a half and presented in either a waffle cone or cone-shaped bowl.

Of course, this being a coffeehouse, their fascination with beverages borders on the obsessive. On the caffeinated side, they'll serve you anything from a cup of regular Joe to one of their steamy, chocolate-laden namesakes. For something a little healthier, they'll whip up a vegetable or fruit juice concoction—your recipe or theirs—for $3.

MOCHA is also a good stop for brunch or a light dinner, particularly if the weather's cooperating and you can snag a seat on the patio overlooking the street. Leading the way are a handful of waffle and pancake choices (green apples, pecans); these run less than $5, and can be supplemented by grilled potatoes, smoked turkey sausage or cinnamon apple slices for another couple of bills. Sandwiches of note include the curried tuna salad and the baked turkey with their cranberry mayo. If you're looking to feed your inner child (or your actual one), $3 will buy you a grilled PB & J, with or without bananas.

COFFEE:

BLACK AS THE DEVIL,

HOT AS HELL,

PURE AS AN ANGEL,

SWEET AS LOVE.

Charles Maurice de
Talleyrand
(1754-1838)

MONTEREY JACK'S
SANDWICH COMPANY
SANDWICHES

Monterey's is located across the parking lot from what is affectionately known in these parts as the Disco Kroger—so dubbed for its proximity to Limelight (now Rupert's), once the king daddy of mid-eighties cheesy nightclubs. Whatever sins of ornamental excess were visited upon that establishment are notably absent here; the sparse decor is comprised of generic-looking tile, formica and plastic foliage. The stripped-down atmosphere is in stark contrariety, however, to the well-stacked sandwiches, which routinely make their way onto those goofy "Best Of Atlanta" lists local publications are forever trotting out.

With more than 50 numbered selections—they'll also build you a custom model—the decision can be a pleasantly vexing one. The Italian combos, made with the likes of peppery capicolla, dry salami and provolone, are quite striking, as is Jack's Smokehouse Special (smoked turkey breast and ham with jack cheese). A goodly percentage of the sandwiches are infused with a decidedly California influence, which is really just a highfalutin way of saying bean sprouts and avocado wedges are in profusion.

Regular sandwiches run about $4, with larges costing more like $7. Each day they feature a couple of different sandwiches along with chips, a soda and a cookie for $5. The choice of breads is broader than you'll find most places, ranging from rugged hoagie loaves and flaky croissants to

3330 PIEDMONT ROAD
BUCKHEAD
404-233-8020
11A-5:30P MON
11A-7:30P TUE-SAT
V/MC

IF THERE WERE NO SUCH THING AS EATING, WE SHOULD HAVE TO INVENT IT TO SAVE MAN FROM DESPAIRING

Dr. Wilhelm Stekel
(1868-1940)

marbled rye and onion rolls. Unless you intercede, the well-synchronized assembly team will pile on shredded lettuce, sliced tomatoes and onions, kosher dills and mild banana peppers, along with some phenomenal dark mustard and a shake of salt and pepper.

NUEVO LAREDO CANTINA

MEXICAN

1495 CHATTAHOOCHEE AVE.
NW ATLANTA
404-352-9009
11:30A-10P MON-THU
11:30A-11P FRI
12P-11P SAT
V/MC/AMEX

Deep in the industrialized heart of Northwest Atlanta you'll find this anomalous Mexican outpost, a quaint and colorful little treasure amid the Sierra Madre of box factories and tool-and-die shops. The name of the game is from-scratch Mexican cooking, done with much style but, as befits the setting, little fanfare. And if you're wondering how it is that the beverage that built this town—Coca-Cola—is nowhere in sight, take note that many of their regulars work at the Pepsi Bottling Plant across the street.

The yellow-and-red, stone-and-brick exterior has a merriness about it, and inside you'll find a motley assortment of bullfighting posters, illuminated pictures of the Madonna with child, and some half-man, half-animal wooden masks. Smokers should head for the downstairs Cadillac Room (adorned with photos and paintings of America's favorite gashogs), which accommodates lit tobacco in the form of cigarettes only. Once you take a load off, you'll be set up almost immediately with a metal bowl of their thick, cilantro-packed salsa and a pile of freshly fried tortilla chips.

Tamales are a strong suit, as are the tacos: crispy and packed with ground beef, finely shredded cheddar, diced tomatoes and mild chiles. The large burritos are somewhat unusual, smothered in a thick cheese sauce and jammed with celery, tomatoes, sweet green peppers and roasted chicken (white and dark meat).

If you're having supper, give the outstanding house specialties ($8-$9) a hard think. Of note are the Chicken Laredo (half a bird spice-rubbed and broiled, with jalapeno-spiked mashed potatoes alongside); a mezmerizing barbecued brisket; and the fajita-style Cadillac Crabcakes, with a white cheese sauce. Entrees are served with fluffy Spanish rice and bland refried beans that almost resemble porridge in consistency.

THE OK CAFE
ECLECTIC SOUTHERN

Like an old country roadhouse hopped up on amphetamines, The OK Cafe is a 'round-the-clock diner that draws you in with neon promises of "Good Food" and a reputation for enormous portions. And because of its proximity to Atlanta's fashionable Buckhead/West Paces Ferry community—and the fact that you can't make reservations—many are the night when the waiting area is a hobnobber's dream, with neighborhood residents like Braves GM John Schurholtz hunkering beside the masses on the long upholstered bench.

1284 WEST PACES FERRY ROAD NW ATLANTA
404-233-2888
OPEN 24 HOURS
V/MC/AMEX

HUNGER AND SELF-
GOVERNMENT ARE
INCOMPATIBLE.

ALDOUS HUXLEY

Brave New World
Revisited (1958)

Whether you sit at the hypertensive counter, watching the short-order magicians ply their craft, or grab a a huge cushy booth, you'll find yourself amid a swirl of multi-medium folk art strung from the walls and ceiling. Waitresses are outfitted in the style of *Alice*, sharp as tacks and generally quite chipper. They'll inform you of any specials; on weekend mornings, keep the radar on for the throughly enticing salmon filets with hollandaise. The Sunday brunch is magnificent and usually damn crowded, but worth the battle. You'll find stacks of hotcakes studded with Granny Smith apples or freshly roasted pecans, along with mammoth three-egg omelets and moist biscuits with blackberry preserves.

At lunch, you'll do well with the plump burgers ($4.95 for the basic model) and any of the big salads. The latter are built upon a foundation of seasonal greens and are quite the eyeful, led by the fried chicken version, topped with almonds and a creamy ginger dressing. Among the plate lunches, the mainstays are roast turkey and cornbread dressing, an incredible pot roast and a chunky chicken pot pie.

The lengthy veggie list (you pick two) is highlighted by slow-cooked black-eyed peas, their renowned six-cheese macaroni, and an airy yellow squash souffle that's downright fantastic. You'll also find a strong selection of shakes and floats ($2-$3) along with hot apple strudel, Boston cream pie and strawberry shortcake—any of which can leave you with a newfound appreciation for the concept of elasticized jeans.

ON THE BAYOU
CAJUN

The South Atlanta municipality of Hapeville—Happyville, the natives call it—is not exactly a tourist destination. Besides being home to the world's busiest airport, Hartsfield International, its distinguishing features are a Ford assembly plant and an awful lot of railroad tracks. While not the sort of environs likely to conjure images of stumpy swamps, moss-strewn trees and Mardi Gras, it's also the unlikely location of On the Bayou, a purveyor of authentic Cajun and Creole eats.

627 NORTH CENTRAL AVE.
HAPEVILLE
404-209-0309
10:30A-8P MON-THU
10:30A-9P FRI
11A-9P SAT
NO PLASTIC

Though the neighboring transmission shop is protected by razor cord and snarling Rottweilers—why, we're not sure—On the Bayou is bright and inviting, the walls covered with Keith Haring-inspired murals and the air buzzing with zydeco tunes. Most everything on the menu is $4 or less, and if you have difficulty deciding which way to go, they'll cheerfully provide you with a taste of anything they're offering that day.

Though they use turkey instead of chicken, the fine gumbo otherwise sticks pretty close to the traditional form: a dark stock populated with whole shrimp, okra, andouille sausage, green peppers and onions. As are all the other entrees, it's ladled generously over a bed of steamed rice. Other menu highlights include the seriously thick jambalaya (with sausage, turkey, rice and veggies); the shrimp etouffee; and a terrific red beans and rice, teeming with scallions and served with Italian sausage.

When crawfish are in season, they get a fresh batch hauled up from the Gulf every Friday in time for dinner. They usually have plenty through the weekend, but every day after that is a roll of the dice as to whether they'll have any left. They're usually about $4 a pound, served up in the boiled, no-frills manner preferred by Cajuns. To eat them, just pop off the heads, suck out the juice and then start to work on the meaty tails. For dessert, their bread pudding has a pleasing density, along with a hardy rum sauce.

PAPA NICK'S
GREEK

1799 BRIARCLIFF ROAD
EMORY AREA
404-875-9677
11A-9:30P MON-THU
11A-10:30P FRI-SAT
4:30P-9:30P SUN
V/MC

In an attempt at working two sides of the Mediterranean, Papa Nick's offers up Italian pizzas along with an assortment of traditional Greek fare. In this they are quite successful; however, in striving to recreate the feel of a Greek cottage they are, as you might envision, considerably less triumphant, with a fake picket fence out front and fake windows painted on the interior walls.

Pizzas are slightly thicker than the ones at Athens Pizza, and they come piled higher than a

> THERE ARE CRAWFISH (OR CRAYFISH, OR CRAWDADS) ALL OVER THE COUNTRY, BUT OUTSIDE OF LOUISIANA THEY ARE ALL BUT IGNORED—LUMPS OF CLAY LACKING A SCULPTOR.
>
> Calvin Trillin
> American Fried (1974)

beehive hairdo with whatever toppings suit your fancy. The gyro meat-and-feta combination is exceptional, a stroke of cross-cultural genius.

Not surprisingly, the gyros themselves are also outstanding: grilled pitas are stuffed and then stuffed some more with beef or lamb, fresh onions, lettuce, tomatoes, and also cheese if you please (feta or provolone). Tops among the appetizers are the yalantzi dolmathes (steamed grape leaves stuffed with rice and pine nuts, served cold) and the spanakopita (seasoned spinach tucked inside feathery fillo dough).

There are also some bodacious Greek dinners, including moussaka (baked eggplant layered with beef and cheese, served with spanakopita, salad and garlic bread) and souvlaki (marinated pork tenderloin that's grilled, topped with feta and served with potatoes or a salad). For the tightest budgets, a huge serving of spaghetti and homemade sauce with garlic bread can be had for under $5.

The best of the five salads is Papa's Classico, strewn with gyro meat and more of that beloved feta ($5.50 buys you a medium, plenty for most folks). And for dessert, they do up an otherwise rarely seen jewel called galatoboureko, fillo pastry filled with thick custard and topped with a hard-hitting honey sauce.

AN EMPTY BELLY KNOWS NO SONGS.
Greek proverb

PASCHAL'S MOTOR HOTEL

MEAT-&-THREE

830 MARTIN LUTHER
KING, JR. DRIVE
DOWNTOWN ATLANTA
404-577-3150
7:30A-11P DAILY
V/MC/AMEX

Long before he entered the national consciousness and garnered a Nobel Prize, Martin Luther King understood the importance of both nonviolent social protest and good fried chicken. While he turned to the writings of Gandhi for ideas on the former, he was known to pop the clutch and lay rubber in the direction of Pashcal's when in quest of the latter. Even after he became world famous, King and his inner circle—many of whom come here still—frequently met to strategize and feast on what has been widely acknowledged as some of the best fried bird in this chicken-crazy town.

Located just down from Morris Brown and Clark-Atlanta universities, on a thoroughfare now named for King, this little hotel run by brothers James and Robert Paschal is a civil rights landmark second and a top-flight Southern eatery first (as lodging, it's a distant third). On any given weekday, you'll have to battle for parking out front or else steer it down the ramp to the lower-level lot—just make sure you don't pull into the two spots reserved for the head honchos or there'll be hell to pay for sure. From there you can take the back stairs and claim a spot either in the smoke-free rear dining room, done up in black and dark reds, or join the tobacco-loving bunch up front.

Foodwise, all roads lead to the skillet-fried chicken, as juicy and tender as you'll find outside of somebody's grandmama's kitchen. If you prefer your poultry baked, opt for the quarter bird served on a bed of cornbread dressing smothered in gravy (served with that curious jellied cranberry sauce). The double-decker grilled ham sandwich is another winner, and the sardine omelet has its diehard fans. Side dishes of note are the edgy collard greens, hunky yams in a buttery syrup, mashed potatoes with a well of brown gravy, and macaroni and cheese. The service can be a bit leisurely, though well-intentioned; you can always pass the time nibbling on their delicate corn muffins and discreetly eavesdropping on the conversations of movers and shakers like Andrew Young, Maynard Jackson and various City Council members.

When it comes to fried chicken, let's not beat around the bush for one second. To know about fried chicken you have to have been weaned and reared on it in the South. Period.

James Villas
American Taste (1982)

Pasta da Pulcinella
ITALIAN

The cool name (pronounced Poo-chin-ella) derives from an unrepentantly adulterous pasta thief in an Italian opera; were the rogue to happen upon this high-ceilinged, low-key eatery, he'd no doubt attempt to pilfer everything in sight. Central to the classy yet dirt-cheap menu are large bowls filled with linguine, ravioli or tagliatelle (a buckwheat noodle that's slightly wider than fettucine), along with fillings and sauces that are the creative equal of any you'll find.

If you're squeezed for time, try a lunch visit before noon or after 1 o'clock, as Midtown office types tend to descend on this place like golden re-

1027 Peachtree St.
Midtown
404-892-6195
11:30a-2:30p,
5p-10p Mon-Thu
11:30a-2:30p,
5p-11p Fri
5p-11p Sat
No Plastic

trievers bearing down on a tennis ball. Worst-case scenario, though, is usually only a brief wait. Whatever the hour, head straight for the cash register, where they apprise you of the hard-to-pronounce ingredients on that day's menu and take your order.

Lunch and dinner portions are the same size and price—about $6 without a salad—and come with a crusty roll. Any of the half-dozen entrees offered are worth a try, but the pizzoccheri coi rapini (buckwheat noodles tossed with garlic,

mushrooms, red peppers and rapini, an Italian vegetable with spinach-like leaves and broccoli-like stalks) and tortelli di mele (round raviolis stuffed with Granny Smith apples, sausage and parmesan, topped with butter and sage) are nothing short of exquisite.

Besides the special pastas, you can also lay your hands on a grand serving of fresh-cranked linguine topped with tomato sauce, pesto or a powerful roasted garlic cream sauce. The linguine is a buck or so cheaper than the others, but figure on seeing the bill escalate if you toss in mixed veggies or smoked chicken. A traditional caesar and terrific house salad comprised of various and sundry fancy greens round out the menu.

THE PITA PLACE
SANDWICHES & PIZZA

Though the Pita Place doesn't always seem sure of what it wants to be when it grows up, it nonetheless manages to wear a number of culinary hats with success. By day it's a sandwich and burger joint, by night a pizzeria serving hand-tossed pies amid an aural backdrop of live music (acoustic stuff, mostly—the Indigo Girls went to high school two blocks away, if that helps you form a mental image). And on the weekends, it's the scene of an extravagant brunch.

Situated directly across from the county court-house, Pita tends to be a bit less crowded than the nearby Crescent Moon on weekends. This is not due to any deficiencies of the brunchtime cuisine, which ranges from the basic breakfast (two eggs, home fries or cheese grits, and a biscuit) to the fine yogurt pancakes or french toast (three huge hunks of challah bread topped with homemade fruit butter) to a create-your-own omelet plan. If you find the latter requires too much thought, try one of their $6 house creations—the mushroom, onion and sun-dried tomato version is especially tasty.

A little further into the day you'll find burgers and chicken sandwiches, both respectable if not earth-shaking and served with either home fries or a salad. If these aren't getting through to you, consider a baked potato with a salad. They do up spuds with style, ranging from the $3 basic model to the rivet-popping deluxe unit ($5), saddled with so much chicken, vegetables, and cheddar cheese you simply have to take their word for it that there's a

127 E. COURT SQUARE
DECATUR
404-370-1111
10:30A-3:30 MON
10:30A-3:30P,
5:30P-11P TUE-FRI
8:30A-3P,
5:30P-11P SAT
8:30A-3P SUN
V/MC/AMEX

AS IT ALWAYS IS WITH CHILDREN, LAST THINGS BEGAN TO RECEDE IN MEMORY AND FOR THE FULL AND GLORIOUS PRESENT, THE THREE SMALLEST PARTRIDGES WERE ALL INVOLVED WITH THEIR HOT DOG, COTTON CANDY AND CORN ON THE COB, RESPECTIVELY. THE TWENTY DOLLAR BILL SHIRLEY HAD GIVEN TO KEITH, AS THE OLDEST CHILD, WAS HEAVILY BITTEN INTO.

Michael Avallone
The Partridge Family
#3: Keith, the Hero

tater underneath. Specialties from the grill include the pita-bound sirloin and shrimp, both grilled with onions, peppers, mushrooms, broccoli, squash, and carrots. In the event that you're practicing your Ugly American routine, you can demand their whopping hot dog—two beef franks on one huge bun, split longways and topped with monterey jack and bacon.

RAINBOW RESTAURANT
VEGETARIAN

2118 N. DECATUR ROAD
EMORY AREA
404-636-5553
10A-8P MON-SAT
11A-3P SUN
NO PLASTIC

Rainbow Grocery dates back to the original days of hippiedom, when the only other option for organic fruits and vegetables and bee pollen was Sevenada, over in Little Five Points. Back then, vegetarians were roundly ostracized in these parts unless they A) had a legitimate medical excuse, or B) hailed from California and were therefore considered beyond redemption anyway. Nowadays, of course, all that has changed, but Rainbow's in-store cafe remains one of the area's premier stops for meatless dining.

Located in the rear of the grocery, the restaurant is diminutive and rather dark, but nonetheless quite comfy. The menu is ever-changing, and you'll find a week's worth of daily specials (usually about $5) listed on a blackboard outside the store. Those dishes exhibiting an Italian or Mexican influence often come off best, particularly the towering spinach-and-zucchini lasagna and the fat burritos stuffed with kidney beans and basmati rice. In addition to the entrees, there are some nice salads and usually a soup of the day—legumes are

their forte, so look for the lentil or black bean. Anything and everything can be packed up for the road.

If your sweet tooth is throbbing for some attention, they offer up a solid selection of frozen delights. In the event that you abstain not only from meat but dairy as well, Tofutti (a soy-based ice cream wannabe) is at the ready; otherwise, they'll set you up with that most politically correct of desserts, the all-dairy-and-loving-it Ben & Jerry's. After you wind things up, it's worth stopping in at the nearby Wuxtry, an excellent used record store with an especially solid selection of reggae. Could you ever have guessed?

RAJA
INDIAN

Situated opposite Pakistan in the far northwest of India, the Punjab region is known as the epicenter of tandoor cooking. The distinctive clay ovens Punjabis use to prepare an assortment of meats and breads have become perhaps the single most common device in stateside Indian eateries, even those owned by folks from other parts of the Subcontinent. Raja is no exception; here the tandoor cranks all the live-long day, turning out everything from smoky garlic naan to roasted chicken and shrimp dishes that are without rival in the city.

Even on the brightest days, the interior is extraordinarily dark, almost theaterlike. With rousing sitar music pulsing in the background and framed photos of rock stars in evidence, you half expect to find George Harrison and Ravi Shankar relaxing cross-legged, talking shop amid a cloud of

VEGETARIANS HAVE WICKED, SHIFTY EYES AND LAUGH IN A COLD, CALCULATING MANNER. THEY PINCH LITTLE CHILDREN, STEAL STAMPS, DRINK WATER, FAVOR BEARDS.

J.B. Morton
in the London Daily
Express (c. 1965)

2919 PEACHTREE ROAD
BUCKHEAD
404-237-2661
11:30A-2:30P, 5:30P-
10:30P MON-THU
11:30A-2:30P,
5:30P-11P FRI
12:30-3P,
5:30P-11P SAT
5:30P-10P SUN
V/MC/AMEX

Gonesh Number 12. Sad to report, you'll encounter nothing of the kind—just a crowd of hungry souls packed into the 15 or so tiny tables, which seems to be about half again as many as the space was designed to hold.

Weekday lunch specials run about $5 and include a limited selection of curries served with rice and a cup of mild mulligatawny soup. The chicken curry or the khema (ground lamb with peas and potatoes in a thick, dark sauce) are the best of the options. For dinner, specialties of the house are the aforementioned tandoori dishes, led by the chicken, which is marinated in yogurt and spices, as well as a drop or two of dye, which gives it the trademark boiled-lobster-red cast.

Rounding out the supper schedule are various curries, kebobs and terrific biryanis (meat and rice cooked with raisins, nuts and peas). Finally, Indians are as bread-crazy a bunch as you're likely to find outside of, well . . . the South. That said, don't fail to order the paratha (a thin pita-like bread) and/or the poori (the leavened, puffy alternative).

RED LIGHT CAFE
SANDWICHES & PASTA

553-I AMSTERDAM AVE.
MIDTOWN
404-874-7828
5P-2A TUE-THU
12P-2A FRI-SUN
V/MC/AMEX

Try though you might, you won't find a more inviting and comfortable place than Red Light to get a tasty bite on the cheap, quaff a few Anchor Steams and lounge around on garage sale furniture. Factor in the frequent live entertainment—jazz and folk, mostly, with improv comedy every so often—and you've got the sort of place Atlanta restaurateurs have been blindly groping at for years: the full-meal counterpart to a coffeehouse.

The owners have of late put considerable energy into paring the menu, though perhaps distilling is the better term. As a starting point you should consider the nifty pesto boboli or the fruit plate, loaded with huge red grapes, hunks of honeydew, perfect strawberries and other juicy doodads. They tend to get their mitts on some top-grade produce, so the green salads are likewise a strong choice, moistened with their own parmesan vinaigrette.

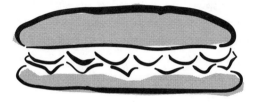

Slightly heartier choices include simple yet substantial sandwiches and a throng of pasta dishes. The tuna melt and the Red Light Club, with ham, turkey, a thinly sliced hardboiled egg and baby-eye Swiss cheese, are both enjoyable; ditto for any of their variations on angel hair noodles, all of which come with breadsticks and a small green salad. They also turn out one heck of a turkey-black bean chili.

More juvenile appetites will find their reward in the $1.75 peanut butter and jam sandwich—if you're looking to be pampered (with a lowercase "P," you'll notice) they'll cut off the crusts and dock you 50 cents. For dessert, be sure to partake of one of their baked items, particularly the chocolate chip cookies or any of the muffins, which come packed with fat blueberries, peanut butter chips—whatever suits the baker's fancy.

A DOG WILL CARRY HIS BONE TO A PRIVATE NOOK AND DO HIS GNAWING UNDISTURBED, BUT CIVILIZED MAN WANTS COMPANIONS WHO CAN TALK, TO NOURISH HIS MIND AS WELL AS HIS BODY.

John Erskine
The Complete Life
(1943)

RIO VISTA
CATFISH

3425 MORELAND AVE.
CONLEY
770-361-0707
11A-9P MON-THU
11:30A-9:45P FRI
1P-9:45P SAT
12P-8:30P SUN
NO PLASTIC

Although the Spanish translation is "river view," the only stream you're likely to see at Rio Vista is if a fellow patron shows up with a leaky radiator. A pastoral scene this ain't, with the surrounding landscape dominated by truck stop parking lots; worry not, however, as any such visual disappointments are more than made up for by the altogether righteous catfish and hushpuppies served on the premises.

As you turn into the gravel lot, you'll no doubt notice that eight of every ten vehicles are American-made pickup trucks (big Fords seem to be the ride of choice these days). It may come as less than a shock, then, to know that smokers are welcome and bleeding-hearts of any stripe are not. Meanwhile, the interior of the 40-year-old establishment looks like, well ... something from 40 years ago. Panelled in dark knotty pine, it's decorated in a style reminiscent of a North Georgia mountain lodge, with all manner of fishing pictures and mounted bass.

THE PICKUP TRUCK IS THE OBVIOUS INSTRUMENT OF CHOICE FOR COOKING SOUTHERN FOOD.

Chris Maynard and Bill Scheller
Manifold Destiny
(1989)

While a flip through the broad menu reveals a platoon of steaks, burgers and fried chicken, those items are rarely seen rolling out of the kitchen. The main attractions, let there be little doubt, are the glorious, cornmeal-coated catfish, so fine they may move the unreconstructed Southern boys in your party to start flicking their lighters and whooping "Free Bird!" A single order (about $6) is a high pile of about eight to ten small whole fish (filets are impractical because of the size), escorted by a crew of hushpuppies and a dish of ice-cold, creamy slaw. Because the fish are on the diminutive side, you'll have to expend some effort liberating flesh from bone, but it's rewarding work. And in true Southern style, they'll keep replenishing your pitcher of iced tea until you plead incontinence.

ROCKY'S BRICK OVEN PIZZA AND PASTAS
ITALIAN

With menu items named after both Vincent Gardenia and Rudolph Valentino, as well as superb pastas and masterfully assembled pizzas, this family-run establishment oozes Italianness at every turn. It has developed a following large and faithful enough to make some churches bridle with envy, the devotees coming to take their meals in a setting characterized by closely packed tables and booths, a wall lousy with photos of famous Italians, and a near-constant din of conversation, hollered instructions and clanking dishes.

Although interesting combinations abound, the 15 specialty pizzas are as sure a bet as there is. Served either Neopolitan- (thin, about $15) or Sicilian-style (thick, $18), the best of this bewitching group includes the elegant pizza bianca (with a sauce comprised of garlic and olive oil, topped with fresh mozzarella, roasted sweet onions and sun-dried tomatoes); the bianca giardiniera (garlic sauce overlaid with hot pepper relish and marinated vegetables); and the cortona (tomato sauce, prosciutto, chicken, artichokes, mozzarella and olive oil).

1770 PEACHTREE ST.
MIDTOWN
404-870-7625
11A-11:30P MON-SAT
5P-11P SUN
V/MC/AMEX

Among the pastas, you should again forego the stock dishes in favor of the specialties, most of which are of Sicilian derivation. Fowl lovers will want to check out the chicken or duck marsala over angel hair or the chicken siciliano (chicken breast, new potatoes, peppers and peas over rigatoni); those with a penchant for things aquatic will find themselves tittering like a schoolgirl at prospects like New Zealand green mussels (over linguine with a garlicky red or white sauce) or the jaw-dropping trout francese.

As a prelude, check out the substantial antipasto plate, or the vegetables di jour—this one rates a must on days when they're doing organic greens sauteed with fresh garlic and olive oil, which you scoop up with hunks of bread. By the end, don't be surprised if you're moved to track down owner Bob Russo and shake his hand—it's akin to falling in love with your therapist.

Savage Pizza

PIZZA

If that old realtor's adage about location, location, location has any merit whatsoever, this gourmet pizzeria doesn't stand a snowball's chance of becoming a franchise. Hooray. Savage is slap in the middle of a sleepy residential neighborhood, next door to Stone Soup Grocery, which Emory grads Sarah Rick and Myron Monsky managed back in the days when it was a grooving health food shop. Then one day, along with pal Field Coxe, they decided to go into the pizza biz, and Stone Soup is now just a regular market, though they still sell spring water for 25 cents a gallon (bring your own container).

IT IS NOT REALLY AN EXAGGERATION TO SAY THAT PEACE AND HAPPINESS BEGIN, GEOGRAPHICALLY, WHERE GARLIC IS USED IN COOKING.

Marcel Boulestin
(1878-1943)

1250 Virginia Ave.
Virginia-Highlands
404-872-2377
11:30a-10p Mon-Thu
11:30a-11p Fri-Sat
12p-10p Sun
No Plastic

Virtually any of Savage's specialty pizzas ($13-$18 for a large) are worth your while. Especially terrific are the Cajun (a red pepper sauce dotted with andouille sausage, shrimp, chicken, onions and green peppers, along with three cheeses); the Mediterranean (garlic white sauce, baked eggplant, artichoke hearts); or the Mai Pai (Canadian bacon, green peppers, red onions, fresh

pineapple). Of course, they also have delicious pizzas of a more traditional sort (whole wheat crust and five different sauces are options), along with $5 calzones (gotta go with the Mexican, jammed full of refried beans, jack cheese and salsa), subs and salads.

The pies here take longer than at most places, but their dedication and attention to detail is deserving of your patience, not to mention respect. Consider the aforementioned red pepper sauce: it involves roasting and hand-peeling a peck (more or less) of sweet red peppers. Much of their business is takeout—mellow location notwithstanding, parking can be a pisser as there are only about six spots total for both businesses—though they have a handful of tables. The waitstaff is generally of the pierce-both-nostrils-and-dye-my-hair-magenta school, though nice enough, and the decor is dominated by Myron's huge murals, which are devoted to celebrating the many adventures of comic book hero Silver Surfer.

SILVER GRILL
COMFORT FOOD

900 MONROE DRIVE
MIDTOWN
404-876-8145
10:30A-9P MON-FRI
NO PLASTIC

This 30-year-old Midtown diner is an oasis of competent Southern food and a shining example of why more restaurants should stick to uncomplicated, reliable menus. Regulars usually pack the place by 11:30 a.m. or so, and since there's no waiting area you can likely end up sweating it out on the sidewalk. Once inside you'll notice that the most recent owners have maintained the throwback feel, with counter seating in front of an open short-order grill and booths running along the front windows, which are treated with floral cafe curtains. In the evenings, the Grill's proximity to the Midtown Promendade (across the street) makes it an especially sweet choice before a late movie or after a twilight show.

If the phrase "comfort food" has an appropriate application, here you have it. Standard downhome entrees are the focus—country-fried steak smothered in gravy and tender, heavily peppered fried chicken, for example—and are supplemented daily by a couple of rotating choices, such as a boneless chicken breast that's butterflied and stuffed with cornbread dressing. Portions are generally ample, though be advised that the grilled pork chops and chicken are a little less satisfying in this regard. The regular selection of vegetables runs along the lines of whipped potatoes and slow-simmered green beans, and it's augmented by a curious crew of specials—English peas, strawberry custard and pickled beets, to name a few.

Meals run a tad over $6, which includes a drink as well as a basket of miniature corn muffins and dinner rolls. If you're feeling ravenous enough to run with the big dogs, double meat portions can be had for an extra $2.50. If on the other hand meat ain't your thang, the vegetable plate (choice of any four) is yours for a five dollar bill. If the dessert mood strikes, opt for a dish of cobbler, made with apples, cherries or, by God, peaches. This is Georgia, after all.

Silver Skillet
Little Skillet
Comfort Food

With its bold green and orange booths, the Skillet looks much as it did when it opened in 1956. That frozen-in-time charm has proved a magnet for more than a few cinematic types, who have frequently used it as a setting for movies and music videos. Despite these intermittent brushes with fame, though, owner Theresa Breckenridge, who took over from father George in 1988, has thankfully remained true to the Skillet's primary mission of doling out memorable Southern plate lunches at reasonable prices.

Though in the broader sense this is two restaurants in one, they share a kitchen and have essentially the same menu (the breakfast offerings differ slightly). The only real distinction, though, is that the Silver Skillet doesn't allow smoking and

AVOID FRIED MEATS, WHICH ANGRY UP THE BLOOD.

Satchel Paige
How to Keep Young
(1953)

200 14TH ST.
MIDTOWN
404-874-1388
6A-3P MON-FRI
7A-1P SAT
8A-2P SUN
V/MC/AMEX

the Little Skillet does. Either place, tables are furnished with a blank ticket and a couple of nubby pencils for you to jot down your selections from the large menu tacked over the lunch counter. You can't go far wrong with anything on the list—the turkey and dressing, country-fried steak, meatloaf and pot roast (all about $5) are all excellent, as are the occasional surprises, most notably the pan-fried lemon-pepper catfish.

For your two vegetables, you'll have about 15 choices on any given day; among the more alluring options are baked sweet potatoes, steamed cabbage, green beans, and mashed potatoes doused with a smooth brown gravy. Meals are also served with light biscuits and corn muffins. And if you can make it fit, try the banana pudding or one of their freshly baked cobblers (peach or blackberry). If you're looking to pass some time while digesting, stroll across the parking lot to the public access cable TV station and grab a seat in the audience of *Talkin' Teens with Marsha* or *The Muslim Roundtable*.

Son's Place
SOUL FOOD

For more than 50 years, Lendell "Deacon" Burton drew a remarkably diverse crowd of businessmen and blue collars, politicians and street people with his rousing combination of lunchtime evangelism and thumping fried chicken. But, with his death in 1993, a dispute arose as to his restaurant's rightful heir; much legal wrangling ensued, and in the end the courts ruled that Lenn Storey, who had begun running Burton's Grill in

So JIM HE GOT OUT SOME CORN DODGERS AND BUTTERMILK, AND PORK AND CABBAGE AND GREENS THERE AIN'T NOTHING IN THE WORLD SO GOOD WHEN IT'S COOKED RIGHT . . .

Mark Twain
The Adventures of
Huckleberry Finn
(1885)

100 HURT ST.
INMAN PARK
404-581-0530
7A-4P MON-FRI
NO PLASTIC

'93, was not Deacon's son and thus had no claim to the place. At that news, he handed over the keys and rented the space next door, calling it Son's Place and serving virtually the same menu.

To be precise about matters, the menu is a sort of stripped down version of Burton's' soul food bonanza, but it's a solid paring down that showcases the best offerings. Perhaps the most pleasant surprise is the inexplicably rare hoecake, a griddle-

fried pancake made from cornmeal batter. You'll always find the spiritually uplifting crispy chicken, along with a couple of other entrees—things like fried fish (mostly whiting), and thick, meaty barbecued beef ribs, kept warm in a bath of homemade sauce. Meals are dispensed cafeteria style for the unhurtful price of $5, which includes two vegetables and a glass of tea.

Like the entrees, the vegetable selections are also limited, but are always fresh, always tasty, and often as not prepared with a hamhock. The collard greens, black-eyed peas and green beans all fall into this category, and they are among the best you'll eat. If you're looking for a little more contrast, go with an order of potato salad or creamy cole slaw. And in the unlikely event that the hoecake doesn't satisfy your craving for cornbread, try a big helping of their dressing—it's full of celery and onions and comes doused with steaming chicken gravy. Any and all visits should conclude with a bowl of warm banana pudding, peach cobbler, or a slice of their stellar sweet potato pie.

IF YOU WANT TO BE REAL TECHNICAL ON THE SUBJECT, WHILE ALL SOUL FOOD IS SOUTHERN FOOD, NOT ALL SOUTHERN FOOD IS 'SOUL'

Bob Jeffries
Soul Food Cookbook
(1970)

Soul Vegetarian

VEGETARIAN

879-A Ralph
Abernathy Blvd.
SW Atlanta
404-752-5194
11a-11p Mon-Sat
9a-1:30p, 5p-11p Sun

652 N. Highland Ave.
Poncey-Highlands
404-875-0145
11a-10p Tue-Fri
10a-10p Sat
10a-2p, 5:30p-10p Sun

V/MC/AMEX

Atlanta is one of four cities—Chicago, Washington, D.C., and Tel Aviv being the others—benefiting from the culinary skills of the African-Hebrew-Israelite Community (AHIC) and its commitment to a pork-, beef- and dairy-free diet. Members of the Community, which describes itself as non-religious but with a strong moral code, own and operate Soul Vegetarians in each city, eateries which go well beyond bean sprouts and limp tofu to deliver a satisfying, sans-meat alternative to fast food.

Of particular interest here are the finely crafted soups. The creamy split pea with garlic is a solid default order, but first check on the soup of the day—their lentil is particularly loveable. Best of the sandwiches are the meged yerikot (a minced-potato-and-carrot patty) and the Garvey burger. A tribute to Jamaican leader Marcus Garvey, the latter is made from kalebone, a pleasantly springy substance derived from wheat gluten. If that description calls to mind a scene from *The Absent-Minded Professor*, rest assured that these bad boys taste considerably better than they come across in print. A fiver lands you a platter that includes either french fries or onion rings (both done fresh), and a tiny salad with a zingy garlic dressing.

The crunchy fried tofu with tartar sauce is also a winner, and you can wash it down with the somewhat clinical sounding Ginger Root Drink, a bracing beverage of their own making. The salad plates—garden, carrot, or tofu—taste fine enough, but even the large ($5.75) will leave you wanting more unless you just came from having your stomach stapled.

One way to fill that hole is with dessert, several of which are quite desirable. Soul makes their own brand of non-dairy frozen confection called, with apologies to Calvin Klein, Eternity. It comes in tantalizing flavors such as vanilla pecan, toasted almond and carob. Tasty, very tasty. Scoops run you about a buck and a quarter, shakes about twice that. A slice of deep-dish pie (sweet potato or apple) will also run you about $2.50.

> *HUNGRY MEN HAVE NO RESPECT FOR LAW, AUTHORITY OR HUMAN LIFE.*
>
> **Marcus Garvey**
> **Philosophy and**
> **Opinions (1923)**

SOUTHFORK
SOUL FOOD

This formerly out-of-the-way soul food joint has undoubtedly benefited from its proximity to the Jimmy Carter Presidential Center and the Freedom Parkway, which cut a wide swath from the Downtown Connector through to Ponce de Leon Avenue. The trek to Southfork, once a winding route through residential neighborhoods, is now a breeze. Of course, given their limited capacity for seating and modest stove space, you can pretty well connect the dots as to the downside of their new, higher profile.

Many of the clientele are working folk, and the morning meal gets rolling well in advance of sunrise. It's around 7 a.m., however, that things really begin to heat up; as folks roll in, the cafeteria-style line doesn't really have anywhere to go

737 RALPH
MCGILL BLVD.
PONCEY-HIGHLANDS
404-522-4809
5A-4P MON-FRI
NO PLASTIC

but to curl through the dozen or so tables. That, and $4 or less, are the price you'll pay to feast on some of the best grits in town splashed with redeye gravy; hickory smoked, thick-sliced bacon; and huge from-scratch biscuits. Big trays of scrambled eggs and link sausages are also there for the asking, along with pan-fried salmon filets. A bottomless cup of coffee is included in the price of all breakfast orders.

At about 11 a.m., the crew shifts gears and swaps out the steam trays. On offer are an impressive array of six or eight entrees and about the same number of veggies; say yes to the the fried chicken, meatloaf, bone-in pork steak smothered in green peppers and onions, simmered collard greens, stewed cabbage and candied yams, but miss the thin, tasteless mashed potatoes and the black-eyed peas, cans of which you may spot on your way to the bathroom.

If you're looking to go the whole way, soul food-wise, they also serve pork neck bones and oxtails pretty frequently. A meat-and-three, with yellow cornbread and serve-yourself sweet tea, will run you under $5. Midday entertainment is provided by the televised version of *Days of Our Lives*, as well as the impromptu rendition courtesy of the ladies working the line, whose banter often includes some colorful complaining about the men they know.

SPICED RIGHT BBQ
BARBECUE

During their restaurant's eight-year existence, the gang at Spiced Right has fielded one question more times than they can begin to count: "Is this meat supposed to be pink?" The answer is, in a word, yep. For owners Steve Lelle, Bill Stansell and Gary Lee, the anxious inquiries are simply their little cross to bear; they use a deep brick oven called a smoke ring—somewhat of a misleading name, given that the heat is applied externally and radiates through to the inside—which gives a distinctly rosy hue to the outside of their slow-cooked pork. It can be startling to the uninitiated, but rest assured you're not stepping onto the express train to Trichinosis Land.

That said, get ready to challenge the capacity of your alimentary canal with a buffet so immense, voracious eaters will wish they had the hinged jaw of a boa constrictor. Since the buffet costs roughly the same as the sandwiches ($5, 11 a.m. to 4 p.m.) at lunch, and is about on par with the dinner plates at night ($7 after 4 p.m.), most everyone is happy enough to belly on up to the smorgasbord. As far as volume is concerned high marks are certainly in order, but it pays to look over the side dishes carefully and be picky. The feast includes fine Brunswick stew and cole slaw, along with pretty fair baked beans, potato salad and bread. The beverage list is topped by some great fresh-squeezed lemonade.

Which brings us to the sauces. Spiced Right sidesteps the regional debate regarding which is

5364 LAWRENCEVILLE HWY.
LILBURN
770-564-0355
11A-9P MON-THU
11A-10P FRI-SAT
V/MC/AMEX

WE NORTH CAROLIN-IANS, OF COURSE, KNOW—WE ARE NOT TAUGHT, WE ARE BORN KNOWING—THAT BAR-BECUE CONSISTS OF PORK COOKED OVER HICKORY COALS AND SEASONED WITH VIN-EGAR AND PEPPER PODS. ... ELSEWHERE IN THE SOUTH, CRUDER TASTES SOMETIMES PREVAIL.

Tom Wicker
(1934-)

best by offering just about all of them. Besides a respectable South Carolina mustard-based concoction and a North Carolina-style vinegar solution, they offer the tomato-based sauce most familiar to Georgians. All three come in a range of heat gradations: mild, hot, a still hotter one called the Lilburner, and the Killer. Sauces are sold for home use, ranging from an eight-ounce squeeze bottle to a gallon for $13.50—what the hell, try a little in your gas tank.

STRINGER'S FISH CAMP
CATFISH

3384 SHALLOWFORD RD.
CHAMBLEE
770-458-7145
11A-9P MON-THU
11A-10P FRI-SAT
12P-10P SUN
V/MC

Despite being nowhere near a navigable body of water Stringer's fairly reeks of the fishing life, its setting characterized by a multitude of nets, oars, and randomly placed outboard motors. There's even a wooden john boat leaning against the front of the building, as though some castaway drifted into the parking lot during a flood and just decided to stay. And well he might, had he a yen for deep-fried fish and hushpuppies of nigh on unbeatable quality.

Any inquiry about how the fish are prepared will likely elicit a puzzled look and a retort along the lines of, "Honey, everything we do is fried." Once you're clear on that point, fish sandwiches are the best way to go at lunch—they're served on a toasted hoagie roll with two large battered cod fillets and grilled onions for about $4. Stick with a side of cold corn salad (with mayo and pimentos) or the sweet cole slaw (also mayo-based) for your roughage.

Dinners can quickly escalate into unbridled feasts, which is why they provide you not with napkins but an entire roll of paper towels. At the center of the action you'll find the voluminous, straight-no-chaser catfish platter (under $10), stacked with eight-inch fillets along with sweet, unadorned hushpuppies. The pups are especially tasty when dipped in Jerry's Hot Sauce (bottled in nearby Roswell), which is stocked at every table.

If you're flying solo, grab a stool at the long counter and join in on the conversation while waiting for your food to fry. Or, you can check out the defunct putt-putt golf course next door, the "clubhouse" of which has since been transformed into a Vietnamese restaurant. Only in America.

THIS DISH OF MEAT IS TOO GOOD FOR ANY BUT ANGLERS, OR VERY HONEST MEN.

Izaak Walton
The Compleat Angler
(1653)

SUNDOWN CAFE
SOUTHWESTERN

Sundown is a blessed sanctuary from all that's overpriced and unimaginative in the restaurant world. The basic theme runs in a Southwestern/Mexican vein, but aside from a few mounted steer heads that motif is relatively understated. And at any rate, the breathtaking whiffs of creativity regularly emanating from the kitchen go far beyond any regional limitations.

At lunch, the Sundown crew's considerable gifts are focused in the direction of soft tacos and soups. Tacowise, there's nary a dud in the lot; among the best are the Memphis (chopped pork with jalapeno cole slaw and tequila-spiked barbecue

2165 CHESHIRE
BRIDGE ROAD
NE ATLANTA
404-321-1118
11A-2P,
5:30P-10P MON-THU
11A-2P,
5:30P-11P FRI
5:30P-11P SAT
V/MC/AMEX

sauce), the carnita (pork with salsa, cilantro and onions), and the fish version—whitefish filets dipped in an egg-and-mustard wash, rolled in corn masa and bread crumbs, then grilled and served with poblano tartar sauce and pickled jalapenos. These all run $1.75 each, and you'll likely require at least two.

Before you go to cramming tacos down your piehole like there's no tomorrow, though, you should know that the soups are nothing less than stunning. The Azteca Green Chili, for example, is a sexy work of art, with pork so implausibly tender it barely holds a solid state. The creamy poblano corn chowder and the sublime turnip green soup are every bit its equal. In addition, they prepare a different chili each day; common to them all is a thrilling disregard for orthodoxy, with the crawfish and black bean combo a particular standout.

At dinner, prices elevate to the $8-$14 range. Top-notch starters include a huge poblano pepper stuffed with cheese and deep-fried, and a pan-fried shrimp cake (chopped shrimp, red peppers and yellow corn) topped with cream sauce. As for the entrees, tacos give way to outstanding enchiladas, grilled chicken and salmon, and substantial fajitas. Whatever you decide, do yourself a solid turn by trying a side of the much ballyhooed turnip greens. And be careful not to fill up on the homemade tortillas, which they hand out like they were Tic Tacs.

TAQUERIA LOS RAYOS

MEXICAN

Rare is the restaurant in this town—yea, *any* town—where you'll find spanking new Lexuses (Lexi?) and minivans sidled up alongside purple El Caminos with twice-pipes. Thanks largely to a menu of uncompromising authenticity, this raucous taqueria has what the boys up in marketing refer to as "crossover appeal." Such is its popularity that if you happen by around the traditional meal times—or if the local soccer team has had a winning day—the salsa-punctuated bustle can be downright electrifying.

Adding to the excitement is an open kitchen, best observed from one of the coveted seats at the six-stool counter. Difficult though it may be to enjoy the artistry of skillful tortilla preparation and simultaneously scan the menu, this is the challenge before you. An order of tacos (choice of filling, all excellent) features a trio of soft corn tortillas for $1.50. Their large tortas (sandwiches) are also winners, served on grilled bread and topped with jalapenos, tomatoes, onions, avocado and cheese. Among the best of these are the ham version and the milanesa (steak coated in an egg batter and fried).

The burritos, meanwhile, are unrivaled in this city. For $3.25 you get a huge flour tortilla stuffed with what seems like a pound of meat—the al pastor (pork) and the chorizo (Mexican sausage) are particularly delicious—along with cilantro, onions, tomatoes, cheese and enough hot peppers to

3290 WEST
HOSPITAL BLVD.
CHAMBLEE
770-936-9278
10A-12A MON-THU
10A-4A FRI-SAT
10A-2A SUN
NO PLASTIC

PATRICIANS RELISHED TRIPE IN BABYLON'S GARDENS, PLEBIANS HAVE ALWAYS WELCOMED IT AS SOMETHING GOOD AND CHEAP, AND ALWAYS THE PEASANT COOK HAS TAUGHT THE PRINCE HOW TO EAT IT.

Various authors
Wise Encyclopedia of
Cookery (1951)

soften a horseshoe. If your belly is crying for something a little less conventional, the choices are many: tripa (pig intestines), sesos (pork brains), lengua (beef tongue) and the manly carnaza (beef from a cow's head). All menu items come with a grilled spring onion, a side of thin, hot pepper sauce and a wedge of lime—just like in Oaxaca.

THAI CHILLI

THAI

2169 BRIARCLIFF ROAD
NE ATLANTA
404-315-6750
11A-2:30P,
5P-10P MON-THU
11A-2:30P,
5P-11P FRI
5P-11P SAT
5P-10P SUN
V/MC/AMEX

The Briarvista Shopping Center would be consignable to the towering slag heap of Atlanta strip malls you needn't bother with were it not for two tenants. One is an exceptionally fine, and exceptionally kosher, delicatessen, which has outstanding meats but unfortunately doesn't sell sandwiches. The neighboring Thai Chilli is the other reason to wave off the wrecking ball, and it is home to some of the city's more artfully prepared and reasonably priced Southeast Asian meals.

The menu is extensive but not overwhelming, and as the name alludes they have a liberal hand when it comes to the hot stuff. Among the curries, the $8 chicken panang, simmered in coconut milk with basil leaves and green peppers, and the pan-fried salmon filets in green curry with basil, zucchini and carrots are both outstanding, and like everything else they can be gotten anywhere from mild to searing.

The catfish filets with Thai eggplant in a peppercorn sauce is another fine way to go. Several vegetarian items are done up right, led by the $7 Spicy Veggie (broccoli, mushrooms, cabbage, basil and tofu in a thick chili sauce).

Relative to the other dishes, the noodle and rice possibilities tend to be relatively tame, spicewise, but by no means lacking in flavor. One of their finer efforts in this department is the Pad See-U. Comprised of your choice of meat (or none at all) along with flat noodles sauteed with eggs, broccoli and garlic in a lightly sweet, soy-based sauce, it is tasty to be sure, if more likely to put you in mind of Chinese eats than Thai.

As for the atmosphere, well, you've seen it all before: black chairs, mauve carpet, mirrored tiles. There must be seminars for this decorating scheme or something. Anyhow, the food is the whole story, and word has gotten around; though you can usually walk right in during the week, if you're not here by 7 p.m. or so on the weekends you can be faced with a half-hour wait.

> *THE FLAVORS ARE ONLY FIVE IN NUMBER BUT THEIR BLENDS ARE SO VARIOUS THAT ONE CANNOT TASTE THEM ALL*
>
> Sun-Tzu
> The Art of War (c. 350 B.C.)

THAI OF NORCROSS
THAI

The folks at Thai of Norcross are seemingly a starstruck lot, what with an entire photo album on display commemorating a visit by Bill Cosby and family. There's Bill blowing on his soup . . . a shot of the kids clinking glasses . . . Bill again, having a bite of noodles. How funnnn. And behind the register you'll spy an autographed photo of REM, with drummer Bill Berry proclaiming their food "The Best Thai in Georgia." While that's open to debate, this quirky place—strung with Christmas lights and outfitted with enough bamboo to make a panda feel at home—is certainly capable of greatness on occasion, and the staff is accommodating almost to a fault.

6065 S. NORCROSS
TUCKER ROAD
NORCROSS
770-938-3883
11A-2:30P,
5P-10P MON-THU
11A-2:30P, 5P-11P FRI
5P-11P SAT
12P-10P SUN
V/MC/AMEX

Their provocative lunch offerings (served with fried rice, soup or a spring roll) are prepared fresh and priced to sell at under $5. You can get lit up by the likes of rama beef (in a red coconut curry over steamed spinach), Summer Shrimp (stir-fried with green beans), or chicken cashew, any of which can be fiery enough to have you turning to your companion and gesturing toward your mouth while scrawling "Are my lips still there?!" on a napkin. Marginally tamer (and cheaper) are old favorites like broccoli chicken and sweet and sour pork.

At night, the expanded menu can be appealing nearly to the point of distraction. To narrow things down, take particular notice of the seafood dishes (most $9 or less)—garlic squid, asparagus shrimp and Spicy Squid lead the charge—and the curries, especially the panang (chicken or beef in a red curry with bell peppers, basil leaves and coconut milk) and kang-pah (made with green beans, carrots and zucchini). Large dinner portions of the beef ribs marinated in a honey, soy and garlic solution are also splendid, as are the Wings of Angels—chicken wings stuffed with pork, clear noodles, mushrooms and onions.

THELMA'S KITCHEN
SOUL FOOD

More than a few critics have suggested that Atlanta's Olympic fever amounts to nothing less than a devil's bargain. Your view on that matter may depend largely on whether or not A) you're holding tickets, and B) you stand to make a pisspot of money off the heightened tourist traffic. Unquestionably, though, this already bustling mu-

764 MARIETTA STREET
DOWNTOWN
404-688-5855
7A-4:30P MON-FRI
8A-3P SAT
NO PLASTIC

nicipality has had to make some tradeoffs along the way, one of which was the closing of the original Thelma's Kitchen in order to construct the Centennial Olympic Park. The popular eatery's demise quickly became a rallying cry for local pundits eulogizing the city's ever-eroding "soul." As luck would have it, however, the soul just picked up and moved a few blocks down, past the CNN Center.

The interior's a little fancier now, what with the addition of modern niceties like curtains and paint, but the spot-on recipes remain. The day's offerings are scrawled on a board, which you may want to study before heading down the cafeteria line. Whether you go for the beef ribs, the intensely satisfying chicken and dumplings or the crackly fried chicken, you're going to make out fine and then some.

You'll also want to sample some of Thelma's featherweight biscuits, perfect for swabbing up any leftover gravy. Among the generally terrific vegetables you will likely encounter are hamhock-strewn collard greens along with homemade creamed corn that'll bring you to your knees (in a good way).

A meat and two veggies will set you back $6 or thereabouts, plus another buck and change if you feel like wading around in a bowl of their stupefying peach cobbler. As for the crowd, it runs quite the range, from road crews in their dusty Carharts to prissy councilmen fretting over how they're gonna get the gravy stain out of that $50 tie.

ALL I WANT IS A FEW HAM HOCKS FRIED IN BACON GREASE, A LITTLE MESS OF TURNIPS WITH SOWBELLY IN IT, AND A HUNK OF CORN BREAD AND I'M HAPPY.

Wyatt Cooper
Families (1975)

TORTILLA'S
MEXICAN

774 PONCE DE LEON AVE.
PONCEY-HIGHLANDS
404-892-3493
11A-11P DAILY
NO PLASTIC

Situated across from a depressing, end-of-the-line strip club, this no-frills Cal-Mex joint turns out top quality meals for bottom dollar. Unlike some other Mexican-inspired eateries around town that pride themselves on their innovative cuisine—Sundown Cafe, for example—these guys play it straight. They concentrate on burritos, soft tacos, quesadillas and little else, done up with fresh ingredients in a simple, elegant fashion. Beyond that, they could give a damn about creativity.

The $2 burritos come loaded with savory pinto beans, jack cheese, rice and salsa. For an extra buck or so, you get a larger flour tortilla and considerably more in the way of fillings. This elevates the whole enterprise to Super status, and its dimensions to that of a yule log. The $2 soft tacos, meanwhile, are wrapped in two corn tortillas, and the quesadillas ($1.55) are grilled flat and leaking cheese. As far as fillings are concerned, they offer a list ranging from green chile peppers on up to chicken, pork, steak and even shrimp. Auxiliary tidbits like chopped tomatoes, onions and cilantro are tossed in as per your instructions.

THERE'S NO WORSE LIFE FOR A MAN THAN TO TRAMP IT. IT'S THIS DAMNED BELLY THAT GIVES A MAN HIS WORST TROUBLES.

Homer
Odyssey (c. 800 B.C.)

Once you place an order and pay at the counter, they'll give you a brightly colored Fisher-Price or Little Tikes toy so the server can spot you. Then you're off to start hovering for a table. On all but the hottest days—beware, they have no air conditioning—it can be a kick to sit upstairs in the smoker's perch and survey the litany of characters who make their way down Ponce at all hours.

TOUCH OF INDIA

INDIAN

The 1995 closing of Brother Juniper's left a dull ache in the hearts of the Midtown lunch crowd, but when it was announced that the renovation of Margaret Mitchell's wobbly house would bump Touch of India off the block, panic set in. Though a fine restaurant disappeared, things still turned out well enough in the end, with *Gone With The Wind* fanatics getting their shrine and Touch of India moving into the old space where Brother J's had dispensed healthy fare for decades.

As is often the case with Indian restaurants, the menu here is by and large an a la carte affair. Lunch is usually a good way to bypass this annoying tendency, and such is the case at Touch of India: for less than $5 you can get a three-course midday special (it changes daily) which includes an appetizer and dessert. As regards the latter, you should be on the lookout for their coconut and pistachio bar, which is quite tasty and only mildly sweet—at least by Indian, or for that matter, Southern standards.

Ah, but we're getting ahead of ourselves. Among the savory lunch options to think about are the mouth-watering kashmiri dishes (chicken or beef simmered with almonds, raisins and bananas in a rich masala) and the excellent vegetable curry. Tandoori dishes, which only come out at dinnertime, are also top-notch. The boti kebab (skewer-cooked lamb) is particularly impressive.

Whichever direction you head, order up some naan ($2), a supple, slightly smoky flatbread that's

962 PEACHTREE ST.
MIDTOWN
404-876-7777

2955 NORTH DRUID
HILLS ROAD
TOCO HILLS
404-728-8881

11:30A-2:30,
5:30-10:30 MON-SAT
V/MC/AMEX

A FULL BELLY MAKES
A HEAVY HEAD.
Indian proverb

cooked in the tandoor (a traditional clay oven). It's a sprawling thing, big enough to split with one or two other people. If you like mango, splurge for a lassi. It is a wonderfully refreshing, shake-like beverage—I'm sounding like Tommy Lasorda here—made with butter culture, yogurt, fruit and a dash of cardamom.

TRIBECA CAFE
CALIFORNIA CUISINE

2880 HOLCOMB
BRIDGE ROAD
ALPHARETTA
770-640-5345
11:30A-2:30P,
5P-10:30P TUE-SAT
V/MC/AMEX

As the unrelenting development of north Fulton County continues apace, the area's restaurant market has become saturated with chain establishments. That being an all too common reality these days, it's nice to know that a small-time, quality eatery like Tribeca can still thrive on its merits. Its main virtues are gourmet food and superior service, not to mention the largest wine bar in the city (more than 60 vinos served by the glass) and a back room that's been transformed into a five-hole putting green so you can practice your short game until your table's ready.

Foodwise, they are unrivaled in the area. Lunch revolves around a nucleus of foccacia, inventive sandwiches (such as the grilled chicken on pita topped with avocado and melted havarti cheese), and salads dressed with balsamic vinegar or a poopy-seed-laced concoction. In the evening the appetizers get big play, led by the peel-and-eat Cajun shrimp and the baked brie in pastry with a strawberry and onion sauce that's loaded with tarragon. Among the main courses, any of the seafood or chicken dishes are worthy of your affections; first among equals are the macadamia-crusted salmon and the Wine Country Chicken.

Their pizzas (12-inchers run $10 or so) are altogether elegant, and they feature the sort of pretty boy ingredients most of us like to crack wise about only to then inhale them like we've never heard the word "silverware." Especially fetching are the New Orleans (andouille sausage, jalapenos and goat cheese), the Southwestern (topped with cheddar, monterey jack and homemade salsa) and the smoked salmon version (with onions and capers).

For dessert, owner Donna Petrucci has her kitchen staff whip up a different creme brulee nightly, made with things like raspberry, mango, or a liberal splash of bourbon. They're spendy ($4.95), but, as Woody Allen once said of orgasms, the worst one I ever had was right on the money.

THE VARSITY
BURGERS AND DOGS

The original Varsity (downtown) claims to be the world's largest drive-in restaurant, and by any measure it stands as an Atlanta landmark. A beacon to America's twin penchants for fast food and unabashed tackiness (not to mention angioplasty), it beckons folks from all walks to belly up to the huge red counter and hear the familiar "What'll ya have?," barked ever so indifferently. So whether you're drawn by the hot dogs (strafed with mustard unless you specify a "naked dog"), those unrepentantly greasy onion rings and fries, or the baby-aspirin-flavored Frosted Orange, rest assured you'll have plenty of company.

So many folks have utilized the Varsity as a meeting place before sporting events that it has be-

61 North Ave.
Downtown
404-881-1706

1085 Lindbergh Drive
NE Atlanta
404-261-8843

6045 Dawson Blvd.
Norcross
770-840-8519

8a-11:30p Sun-Thu
8a-1:30p Fri-Sat
No Plastic

come as much of an Atlanta tradition as, well, seeing the Falcons receive their yearly ass-whippings courtesy of the 49ers. In addition to the dozen or so indoor dining rooms (each with its own TV, all tuned to different channels), the original drive-in area remains. It can hold perhaps 20 cars, and is patrolled by servers who'll wait patiently beside your car until you realize you forgot to tip them.

Up on the enormous menu board you'll find all manner of cholesterol-intensive fare, much of it quite tasty if somewhat likely to provoke feelings of self-loathing. The chili slaw dogs are quite the rage, but they also have the predictable assortment

of sandwiches (egg salad, pimento cheese, and so on) and, of course, burgers (have 'em slap some chili on that thing). For dessert there are brownies, fried fruit pies, and frozen yogurt, looking about as out of place as Newt Gingrich in a leotard.

Though quantity and quality obviously don't always travel in the same buggy, it's hard to help being awed by the Varsity's stats: on each of the 365 days they're open, they reportedly go through an average of two miles of hot dogs, a ton of onions, 2,500 pounds of potatoes, 5,000 fried pies and more Coca-Cola than any other single establishment on the planet.

VIETNAMESE CUISINE

VIETNAMESE

3375 BUFORD HWY.
NE ATLANTA
404-321-1840
11A-11P DAILY
V/MC/AMEX

While the setting and rather unimaginative name might not suggest authenticity, Vietnamese Cuisine is in fact, like the nearby El Salvador, a compelling book cursed with a lackluster cover. For, once inside, you'll discover a clean and comfy dining area with flowery wallpaper and linen tablecloths, as well as a doting staff more than willing to help first-timers get a handle on the extensive menu.

To kick things off, try either the bo cuon (beef with rice vermicelli and vegetables in rice paper) or the popular cha gio, a rice paper rollup that's stocked with vegetables and fried—a slightly more delicate cousin to the spring roll, essentially. A wide variety of terrific soups are on offer; you can't go wrong with either the canh cai thap cam (veggies with shrimp and pork, $12 for two, $6 for one); or any of the pho selections.

Pho (under $5) is a delicate and aromatic traditional soup featuring beef, rice noodles and plenty of fresh herbs. It's usually eaten as a meal in itself, not as an accompaniment, and can be had in a dozen or more variations. Probably the most common add-in is round steak, sliced whisper-thin, but other options, in combination or alone, include flank steak, tendon, and tripe.

Some of the best ideas for a non-soup order include bo xao xa ot (stir-fried beef with hot chili peppers and onions); ga xao Saigon (tender stir-fried chicken and vegetables); and the literal and figurative mouthful tom xao dua leo chua ngot (call it sweet and sour shrimp, with onions, cucumber and tomatoes). Beveragewise, order the coffee drink beside which all others pale: espresso with condensed milk. You can get it hot, but iced is the preferred medium. After dinner, try the flan cake ; or, if the meal's left you full to busting, you can always just stick with the small Tootsie Roll they give you on your way out.

VINNIE'S
BURGERS

1459 SCOTT BLVD.
DECATUR
404-373-7766
11A-3A DAILY
V/MC

This campy salute to all-American burger joints puts on a spread of which the *Happy Days* gang might only have fantasized. Just think what a happening place Arnold's would have been had they installed a full bar in the back room and declared Tuesday as Ladies' Night. That's the lay of things at Vinnie's, and they even prime the pump with schnapps shots for a buck. Ain't life grand?

The reliable menu rests on a solid foundation of sandwiches ($5 or so), most notably the hand-pressed burgers, steak hoagies, chicken breast subs and gigantic turkey sandwiches—"gigantic" referring here to the sandwich, not the bird. If you appreciate a nicely done link, they come through with scrumptious sausages of both Italian (topped with sauteed onions and sweet green peppers) and Polish extraction (smothered in kraut and spicy brown mustard).

Not surprisingly, the list of snacks and side orders is populated with many a deep-fried item, though they also have corn on the cob and a few salads. Pay special attention to the blistering chicken wings, as well as the battered zucchini strips—ah now, what would our boy Potsie make of these?—served with their "breath-enhancing" garlic sauce. The home fries, grilled with onions, bell peppers and garlic, are also excellent.

To wash it all down—Joanie, Chachi, cover your ears, please—Vinnie's offers draft beer. Not an import in sight, mind you; closest they come is Rolling Rock, from , umm . . . Pennsylvania. Booze-by-the-pitcher can be had in the form of Long Island iced tea, margaritas and the ironically named Lucid Lemonade (made with bourbon). Before you go scheming to re-enact a few scenes from *The Lost Weekend*, however, take note that these are only served to parties of two or more.

VIRGINIA'S
COFFEEHOUSE

Set back among the old brick apartment buildings on the east edge of Virginia-Highlands, this little coffeehouse exudes a casual, somewhat cerebral, charm. The patio area is especially inviting, but if the weather or a dearth of seats forces you indoors, you'll find exposed brick, oriental rugs and a rotating assortment of artwork and photographs. Atop each of the dozen wooden tables sits a thick glass candle bearing the image of a little-known saint. If you're by yourself—or not, and wishing you were—they subscribe to a wide variety of American and European magazines, everything from *The Economist* to the *Utne Reader*.

THINK OF THE MAN WHO FIRST TRIED GERMAN SAUSAGE.

Jerome K. Jerome
Three Men in a Boat
(1889)

1243 VIRGINIA AVE.
VIRGINIA-HIGHLANDS
404-875-4453
4P-11P MON-FRI
10A-11P SAT-SUN
NO PLASTIC

Basic espressos start at $1.25 and a pot (a little over two cups) of the java of the day is the same price. They offer the widest selection of teas in town (nearly 40), served by the pot—you can choose from the likes of lychee black, mango or the decaf honeysuckle. A litany of other drinkables is at the ready, ranging from fresh strawberry lemonade to hot milk with anisette.

The food menu is all over the map, with something of an Indonesian slant. Appetizers of note include the peanutty chicken skewers served with a small toasted baguette ($5.50) and the baked brie in pastry topped with raspberry preserves. The soups generally warrant high marks, though none can compare with the Caribbean Chicken Peanut Stew—sadly, it only appears intermittently. If you're looking for more of a meal, the black bean burger and the regular beef model are worth knowing, as is the turkey and Swiss sandwich, heaped with Roma tomatoes and swabbed with honey mustard and pesto.

In the coffeehouse realm, of course, desserts often constitute a full meal. Virginia's has some accomplished bakers on staff who routinely turn out a bevy of toothsome choices, including apple or blueberry pie (complete with latticed top), profiterole au chocolat (puff pastry crammed with vanilla ice cream and topped with warm chocolate sauce), and a delicious strawberry shortcake.

A REAL ART STUDENT WEARS COLOURED SOCKS, HAS A FRINGE AND A BEARD, WEARS DIRTY JEANS AND AN EQUALLY DIRTY SEAMAN'S PULLOVER, CARRIES A SKETCH BOOK, IS DESPISED BY THE REST OF SOCIETY, AND LOAFS IN A COFFEE BAR.

John Bratby
Breakdown (1960)

THE VORTEX
BURGERS & BEER

Situated across the street from a cable TV company, The Vortex is known for its excellent hamburgers, vast beer selection and curmudgeonly attitude—not always in that order. The well-worn chestnut about the customer always being right doesn't fly too high here, nor do the notions of fast food, menu substitutions  or political correctness. The atmosphere is tempered with a proper amount of humor, though, and the food is top-notch, so don't be bashful about sliding in to either the nicotine-friendly main room downstairs or the allegedly smoke-free upstairs loft—umm, shouldn't that be the other way around? Don't ask.

With an almost suffocating collection of flea market curios and castoffs—everything from a giant Felix the Cat to a dwarfish airplane to a hazardous waste barrel—this place is a feast for the eyes. For feasting of a more sustaining sort, you'll find a bewitching roster of half-pound burgers ($5-$6 with fries or potato salad), which come in about a dozen different get-ups. Among these are a grilled patty coated with a mouth-numbing jerk potion percolating with allspice, thyme and habanero peppers. For a truly fascinating Southern beef experience there's the Pimento Cheeseburger; the tasty Santa Fe (melted jack and cheddar cheeses and homemade salsa) is not a bad way to go, either.

1041 W. PEACHTREE ST.
MIDTOWN
404-875-1667
11:30A-2A MON-FRI
6P-2A SAT-SUN
V/MC/AMEX

Other sandwiches to watch for include a nicely done chicken breast, some hefty bratwursts, and a swanky turkey reuben. Lighter appetites may find soup to be sustenance enough, particularly if you get here on a day when they're ladling up corn and asparagus chowder. The black bean is pretty strong as well, and always available. Of the 100 or so different brewskis on hand, you'll find taps flowing with both Whitbread Ale and Guinness Stout.

WHITE HOUSE RESTAURANT
MEAT-&-THREE

On first pass, White House can be a little difficult to spot amidst the yuppie glitter of Buckhead. The high-rent location can also make parking a challenge, and you'll pay about a dollar more than the going rate for a meat-and-three (two, actually); but these are trivial concerns when set beside this Greek-owned, Southern-style eatery's considerable culinary attributes.

Round about noontime, it's almost a certainty you'll find the place abustle with hungry folks and scurrying waitresses. If jockeying for a spot in the 20-table dining room is bumming you, you can always hit the counter up front for takeout. The counter also provides an opportunity to get up to speed on the specials of the day.

These typically number about a dozen or so ($6), and include reliable fare like grilled pepper steak, chicken and dumplings, dainty crab cakes (damn good, believe it or not), meatloaf, and spaghetti (a fave of many regulars). The cornbread, with a super-moist cakey texture, is unusual and

3172 PEACHTREE ROAD
BUCKHEAD
404-237-7601
6A-3P MON-SAT
8A-3P SUN
NO PLASTIC

delicious. Any of the open-faced sandwiches (sided with fries or mashed potatoes) have the capacity to set your world right.

Although lunch draws the biggest crowds, White House serves fine breakfasts any time, ranging from two-egg combinations to hotcakes and omelets (most $5 or under). The Working Man's Breakfast contains a couple of eggs, a pork chop, biscuits and grits for just over $5 (an extra chop is yours for two bills). Dinner specials follow more of a Greek-theme, most notably in the form of a gyro platter and the humongous Greek salad, littered with anchovies and feta cheese. For dessert, get busy with the homemade blackberry cobbler, carrot cake or lemon icebox pie.

A MAN IS IN GENERAL BETTER PLEASED WHEN HE HAS A GOOD DINNER UPON HIS TABLE, THAN WHEN HIS WIFE TALKS GREEK.

Samuel Johnson
Boswell's Life of
Johnson (1773)

WILLIAMSON BROS. BAR-B-Q

BARBECUE

Though the brothers Williamson received national attention when they catered a party for a certain local politician when he was named top dog in the U.S. House of Representatives, Danny, Marty and Larry have long been celebrities in the barbecue world. They've forged a reputation for excellent chopped pork, and have become to catering what the Grateful Dead were to touring; it is their milieu. If you can't catch them out and about, though, their Marietta establishment is no slouch, with its tin roof, log cabin exterior, rocking chairs on the front porch, and hickory smoke forever billowing from the chimney.

Smack in the middle of this huge restaurant sits a barbecue pit, manned by a sweaty guy armed

1425 ROSWELL ROAD
MARIETTA
770-971-3201
10:30A-9P MON-THU
10:30A-10P FRI
10:30A-9:30P SAT
V/MC/AMEX

with a sauce-soaked mop for basting ribs. If you're dining in, there's no beating the all-you-can-eat deal on pork and chicken; it runs about six bucks, and includes garlic toast and side dishes. For lunch on the go, you can keep things cheap by getting a jumbo pork sandwich served on a discus-sized bun, sided with a dish of sweet cole slaw and a bowl of their sassy barbecue beans. Williamson's version of Brunswick stew is a masterful spin on the traditional recipe—brimming with pork, corn and black pepper, it has the thick, translucent consistency of hot and sour soup.

If you're of a mind to treat yourself, the ribs are a superb dinner option: a slab with three side dishes runs $14. If you can walk away hungry from this feast, you might as well head straight to the nearest physician and request a full work-up. To finish the job, order a slice of one of their fine homemade pies (chocolate, lemon, coconut or banana). As is often the case at barbecue joints, you can also get whole pies for the road. The restaurant's entryway is a veritable gauntlet of merchandise, with plenty of Williamson Bros. brand barbecue sauce as well as, strangely, their own version of ground black pepper.

WOODY'S
SANDWICHES

With its caboose-inspired architecture and crazy, undulating parking lot, Woody's is tough to miss. Perched in the middle of a three-way interesection, it's within walking distance of the city's largest public green space, Piedmont Park, known for its dog-friendly attitude and fine

It is no exaggeration to say that many a gubernatorial election in Georgia has been carried by means of votes gained at barbecues.

John R. Watkins
in The Strand (1898)

981 Monroe Drive
Midtown
404-876-1939
11a-10p Mon-Sat
No Plastic

rollerblading possibilities. Woody's is a bit cramped (five small booths), but the food is pretty portable—mondo cheese steaks, hearty hoagies and a variety of ice cream-based goodies—and most folks get it to go. If you are eating in, however, you should know that there's no air conditioning, though with the windows open—this place is practically nothing but windows—and the ceiling fans cranked you'll be comfortable enough except on the hottest afternoons.

For about four bucks you can get a cheese steak or plain steak on a soft, fresh French roll baked right here. The tender chipped sirloin is cooked with onions, and topped with bright mustard and ketchup, along with white American cheese if you like. Other subs include a well-stuffed turkey, tuna salad, ham or Italian for about $3.50—get 'em topped with either sweet cherry or hot banana peppers. They also have an Italian sausage with grilled onions and peppers and provolone cheese that's worth knowing about, all the more when capped with a thatch of sauerkraut.

The frozen concoctions aren't anything fancy—everything is made with one or more of the Breyer's mainstays: vanilla, chocolate and strawberry—but they do the trick. Woody's' crew possesses an especially deft touch with shakes and splits, any of which are delightful enough to arouse in you heightened levels of empathy for the lactose-intolerant.

SNATCH AND EAT,
SNATCH AND DRINK,
FOR THIS WORLD IS
LIKE A WEDDING.

Talmud: Erubin
(c. 200 A.D.)

INDEXES
INDEXES
INDEXES

WHO

WHERE

WHAT

Salvadoran

Sandwiches

About the Authors

MARCH EGERTON was raised in Nashville and known for making highly advantageous mealtime trades in the school cafeteria. He has since lived in Chapel Hill, Seattle, Honolulu, and most recently, Portland, Oregon, where he still has dreams about Aunt Velva's fried chicken. This is his fourth book.

STEVE ROSENBERG is a writer and newspaper editor who has lived and eaten in the Atlanta area since 1986. A Nashville native, he was reared on the soul-stirring Southern cooking of, among others, his grandmother, Nannie Mae McCarty, best known for her chess pie and cornbread dressing. Steve and his wife, Donna, have two children and a dog that has yet to miss a meal.